THOREAU

of Walden Pond

NORTH STAR BOOKS

THOREAU
of Walden Pond

STERLING NORTH

Illustrated by Harve Stein

1 9 5 9
HOUGHTON MIFFLIN COMPANY BOSTON
The Riverside Press Cambridge

Books by

STERLING NORTH

Plowing on Sunday
Night Outlasts the Whippoorwill
Seven Against the Years
The Pedro Gorino (with Captain Harry Dean)
Speak of the Devil (with Clip Boutell)
So Dear to My Heart
Reunion on the Wabash
The Birthday of Little Jesus
Abe Lincoln, Log Cabin to White House
Son of the Lampmaker
George Washington
Young Thomas Edison
Thoreau of Walden Pond

HENRY DAVID THOREAU loved the little Concord River the way Mark Twain loved the mighty Mississippi. Rowing, sailing, swimming, and fishing, young Thoreau lived the life all boys love to live.

I too lived that sort of life in my boyhood. Even before I read *Walden* I had built a boat with two masts — not to mention a canoe and a rowboat. In my late teens I also built a cabin of hewn oak logs and limestone on the shore of Rock River in southern Wisconsin. The spirit of *Walden* was there in Wisconsin, also — the sound of a lonesome train whistle rushing through the night, a whippoorwill calling through the dusk, the *tr-r-r-oonk, tr-r-r-oonk, tr-r-r-oonk* of the bullfrogs on the river's edge, and the frequent "roar and pelting" of rainstorms on the tight roof.

However, I viewed nature more perceptively after reading Thoreau, learned to identify scores of additional birds and wild flowers, put away my gun, and wondered how I could ever have been a hunter.

The way to read *Walden* (or any book about Thoreau) is to find a quiet place where you can listen to the music of nature coming to you from the printed page. Take the book outdoors under the same sky Thoreau loved in any season. Take it with you to your camp or cottage. Read it thoughtfully and slowly, savoring each sentence, and you will be surprised to find a great sense of peace and well-being coming over you — the spirit of Thoreau and of the universe.

STERLING NORTH

For GLADYS, my companion

on these and other waters

CONTENTS

It seemed as if the breezes brought him,

It seemed as if the sparrows taught him,

As if by secret sign he knew

Where in far fields the orchis grew.

RALPH WALDO EMERSON

Boyhood on the River

1

THE NEWS SPREAD like wildfire among the boys of
Concord. Canal boat! Canal boat! Hurry or
you'll miss it.

The big boat loaded with casks of lime and
thousands of bricks could be seen "stealing mys-
teriously through the meadows and past the
village . . . as silently as a cloud." The rivermen
poling these large scows were greatly envied by
the Concord boys.

Think of living and sleeping on a boat like that!
Think of knowing every inch of the river for miles
and miles!

Henry Thoreau and his brother John promised
themselves that some day soon they would build

a boat of their own. Then, after the morning chores were done — the cow milked, the chickens fed, and the garden hoed — they could go exploring. Perhaps, when they were older, they might take the trip of which they had dreamed, far down the quiet Concord River to the rushing Merrimack.

In time they built their first boat. It was a crude little craft, but at least it floated. Sometimes it even sailed. Sir Francis Drake scouring

the Spanish Main was no more proud of his *Golden Hind* than were these Concord boys of their homemade boat.

Occasionally they took their older sister Helen and their younger sister Sophia for a sail on the Concord or one of its two branches.

More frequently the boys went adventuring alone. They would cast anchor a mile or more from the village to swim or fish, pick berries, or wild grapes.

Often they played they were savages of the Massachusetts tribe which once had lived along this stream. These brothers were as brown and lean as Indians. They loved the water and the woods.

Years later when John was away from home, Henry wrote: "Brother: it is many suns that I have not seen the print of thy moccasins by our council-fire."

An Indian should know every bird and animal, for these are brothers of the red man. John, who was three years older than Henry, taught him all that he himself knew about nature.

He showed him the grass lodges which the muskrats build.

He pointed out the long-legged blue heron fishing in the shallows.

He taught him to recognize the cheerful "Kon-keree!" of the red-winged blackbird.

One day, however, they saw a bird which John could not identify. And there were many flowers he could not name. Henry realized that even so wise a companion as his brother could not answer all his questions. It would take Henry Thoreau the rest of his life to learn the secrets of nature. But his wonder was first aroused in the days when he and John played Indian, there on the river.

When Thoreau was born in Concord, Massachusetts, on July 12, 1817, James Monroe was President of the United States. Thomas Jefferson, author of the Declaration of Independence, was still alive. Far to the west, in Southern Indiana, an eight-year-old pioneer boy named Abe Lincoln was learning to split rails.

The Thoreaus were not quite as poor as the

Lincoln family, but they were poor enough. On the mother's side, several ancestors had been prosperous Tories who had aided the British in the American Revolution. On the father's side, the Thoreaus had been successful merchants in the Channel Islands, off the coast of France.

But the Thoreaus of Concord seemed to have lost the golden touch. John and Cynthia Thoreau despite their poverty, however, welcomed the arrival of their third child, David Henry (who later reversed his name to Henry David). Certainly the new baby delighted the two older children, Helen and John. Shy little Henry needed the affection of this lively and intelligent family.

Cynthia, the mother of this tribe, was larger and noisier than her husband. In fact she was the most talkative woman in Concord.

John, the father, was rather quiet and fortunately a trifle deaf. He liked to read his paper undisturbed.

After Henry was born in Concord, the family moved briefly to nearby Chelmsford and then to

Boston. In neither of these communities were they financially successful. Even little Henry seems to have sensed the family's poverty because he was made to feel ashamed of his poor sled. "The boys say it is not shod with iron and not worth a cent." He could not whittle a bow and arrow for a friend

because he did not have a knife. But he was rich
in another way — he had the whole world around
him to explore.

By the time Henry was six years of age, the
Thoreaus had returned to Concord where they
would now remain. Here the head of the household became a maker of pencils.

Pencil making takes skill. A black mineral
called graphite is ground into a fine powder.
This is mixed with another substance and molded
into pencil-cores. The cores are then encased in
wood. Look at a pencil and notice the way it is
made — not an easy task! John Thoreau made
tens of thousands of excellent pencils which he
sold for a few cents each. In time he took his sons
into the business and the sign over the shop read:
JOHN THOREAU AND SONS

Still there was little money. So goodhearted,
hard-working Cynthia Thoreau took in roomers
and boarders. Many of these were relatives. Affectionate aunts were plentiful. Far more enter-
taining was Cynthia's brother, Uncle Charles
Dunbar.

Uncle Charles delighted the children of Concord. He could flip his hat in the air and catch it on his head. He did marvelous card tricks. He pretended to "swallow" his knife, fork, and spoon, but would generously return them to his hostess for another helping of chicken. He was gentle, but extremely strong — the best wrestler in miles. He would vault over his yoke of oxen before you could say "Jack Robinson." But his best trick was to balance a twelve-foot ladder, then run up one side and down the other before the ladder could fall.

Uncle Charles was not the only salty and saucy character in Concord. Aunt Mary Emerson, a bright mite of a woman, had a heart that was warm, but a tongue as sharp as a needle. Many farmers and villagers prided themselves on speaking their minds. Peddlers carried not only their packs, but also a store of exciting tales. A boy could learn much if he listened.

The Thoreaus usually kept a cow, fattened a few pigs, raised chickens and turkeys, and fed many contented cats.

The cow must be milked and taken to pasture. The pigs must be chased and caught if they slipped through the fence. But to Henry Thoreau the cats were a pure joy. He would watch a playful kitten by the hour.

He noticed that a kitten chasing its tail might as well be two cats, quite unaware that its front paws are related to its teasing, twitching tail. He liked the way cats purr and bask in the sun.

One reason why Thoreau liked cats was because they are so free, leading their own lives. Thoreau, too, liked to prowl alone through the meadows and the woods like a cat. And like a cat he enjoyed fishing.

Often he was to be seen, knee-deep among the water lilies, fishing for the perch and sunfish which abound in the Concord River. Sometimes, if he was lucky, he hooked a pickerel and had to fight and struggle to bring the big fish ashore. How proud he must have been on those occasions when, barefooted and happy, he trudged home with his pole over his shoulder and his big fish

dangling at his side — a meal for the whole family.

By the time Henry Thoreau was born, life had become a little easier in New England. Many were poor, but none were starving.

It had taken a determined and God-fearing people to wrest a living from the stormy Atlantic and the stony soil. Farmers had to be tough, shrewd, and self-reliant to live through the winter. They had learned to be economical — to "wear it out, use it up, make it do."

Often New England had been torn by war: the Pequot War, King Philip's War, the century of frontier conflict with the French, the American Revolution, and the War of 1812. There was scarcely a community in the whole region which had not lost men in one or another of these struggles. Sometimes whole families had been scalped, and entire villages burned.

Then there was the ceaseless struggle against evil and ignorance. Such constant battles produced lean men with keen minds.

Concord had been more fortunate than many New England villages. To this peaceful valley in 1635 had come about a dozen pioneer families. Land was purchased from the gentle savages. The peace pipe was solemnly passed around. And the new settlement was named "Concord" in memory of this friendly, long-lasting agreement with the local Indians.

The soil here was relatively fertile, with river meadows which produced an abundance of wild hay. The slow-moving stream was alive with fish. Moreover, this town was far enough from the Atlantic so that few of its men were lost at sea. However, no spot on earth is ever completely safe from the danger of war.

On April 19, 1775, Concord was the least peaceful village in North America. Up the road from Lexington came the British Redcoats, bayonets gleaming, drums beating proudly. They were headed for Concord to seize arms and ammunition stored by the colonial forces.

To prevent them, if they could, out rushed the Concord Minute Men with their muskets.

By the rude bridge that arched the flood,
Their flag to April's breeze unfurled,
Here once the embattled farmers stood,
And fired the shot heard round the world.

Emerson of Concord wrote that poem in memory of the first heroes of the American Revolution. And young Henry Thoreau often sailed his boat past the ruins of the old North Bridge where the battle was fought.

In Thoreau's youth, Concord was a town of about 2000 people. Teamsters from New Hampshire and Vermont drove market wagons filled with farm and forest products through Concord to Boston, twenty miles farther down the highway. On their return journey they hauled "West India goods" and other merchandise. Going and coming they stopped at Concord's three taverns.

Except for this traffic, the town was quiet and orderly. There was the church, where Dr. Ripley preached on the Sabbath, lifting its spire above the elm-shaded streets. And along these streets stood houses, painted white or allowed to weather a silver gray.

"The vitals of the village," Thoreau later observed, "were the grocery, the bar-room, the post-office, and the bank; and as a necessary part of the machinery, they kept a bell, a big gun, and a fire-engine, at convenient places."

The Thoreaus, though respected, were not members of the social circle, which included the Emersons and Hoars and Ripleys. Nevertheless, they were well acquainted with these foremost families and took an interest in village activities.

Young Henry, however, cared little for the town itself. This rather quiet boy with prominent nose, striking gray-blue eyes and short, wiry body would rather climb the fence and stride into the woods to pick berries. He liked to swim, skate, and take long hikes. He particularly enjoyed climbing a hill from which he could see Mount Monadnock far to the west. Some day, he promised himself, he would scale that blue mountain and look down upon the world lying far below him.

Even the happiest summer vagabond must put aside his fishpole when autumn comes and the school bell rings. Thoreau, whose family included several schoolteachers, learned his letters at the age of five. By the time he was sent to school, he was reading for pleasure, a wonderful pastime which continued to delight him for the rest of his life.

He was no child prodigy, but he was bright. A composition which he wrote at the age of ten, entitled "The Seasons," shows that he liked the outdoors and enjoyed writing. He starts with a four-line verse:

> Why do the seasons change? and why
> Does winter's stormy brow appear?
> Is it the word of Him on high
> Who rules the changing, varied year?

Henry then moves swiftly through the four seasons, telling of Spring, "green with the newborn grass"; Summer with its "trees and flowers . . . in bloom"; Autumn when "the markets abound with fruit"; and Winter when "the cold is so intense that the rivers and brooks are frozen."

In this little nature essay, Thoreau has chosen to use the seasons as an outline. When as an adult he wrote his masterpiece, *Walden, or, Life in the Woods,* he once again took his reader on a circular tour of the seasons.

As the twig is bent, the tree grows! Thoreau at ten already foreshadowed faintly the talent he would one day demonstrate as America's greatest poet-naturalist of the nineteenth century.

In addition to the opening of school, autumn

brought another pleasure, the annual cattle fair.
When the elms showered their yellow leaves on
the village street, the crowds began to gather.
Then one might hear the lowing of cattle and the
bleating of sheep, and see "a hundred yoke of
oxen" hitched together.

"The wind goes hurrying down the country,"
Thoreau wrote, "gleaning every loose straw in the
fields, while every farmer lad too appears to scud
before it . . ." Here they all came, as though blown
in by the autumn wind, in "best pea-jacket and
pepper-and-salt waistcoat," eager not to miss a
single exhibit at the fair. No wonder Thoreau was
excited by those "stirring autumn days, when men
sweep by in crowds, amid the rustle of leaves . . ."

Concord was not a town, however, to concen-
trate mainly on cattle shows and other spectacles.
It was a rather serious community, more interested
than most in books and education. At the Concord Lyceum, lecturers were to be heard throughout the season. Thoreau began attending these
lectures at the age of twelve, and in later years
delivered some of the lectures himself.

Many of the leading citizens of Concord were Harvard graduates. A Harvard diploma was a "passport to any society." The Thoreaus naturally wanted Henry to prepare for Harvard. He was, therefore, enrolled in the Concord Academy where he was introduced to Latin and Greek.

Thoreau did well at the Academy. But sometimes his mind must have gone wandering down the Concord River or out to Walden Pond where he had been as free as an eagle soaring on the wind, or a fish flashing through the water. There, under the high-arching sky, was Thoreau's real academy, the Academy of the Universe.

2

IN SEPTEMBER of 1833 Henry Thoreau said good-by to his family and took the twenty-mile journey from Concord to Cambridge to begin his first year at Harvard.

Behind him lay the comforting sounds of his native village, the blacksmith's hammer ringing on the anvil, the distant clang of cowbells in the meadows, and the lively chatter of his mother, his sisters, and his aunts.

Ahead of him lay new adventures.

True, he was hungry for knowledge. But Thoreau at sixteen did not feel particularly well prepared for college. Moreover, he was painfully aware of his green homespun jacket, his country

manners, and his lack of pocket money. He knew
however, that he must now square his shoulders
and make his way among strangers.

He did not feel as gay and assured as some of
the young men he saw swinging along the streets
of historic Cambridge. The gracious colonial
mansions of Brattle Street had a pleasant air. But
they reminded this village boy that Cambridge
had been a center of wealth and learning for two
hundred years.

Shy though he was, Thoreau's pulse must have
quickened as he stepped into Harvard Yard with
the September sunlight slanting through the elms
upon the white granite of University Hall, and
upon the ivy-covered brick of Stoughton and
Hollis.

Did Thoreau, who was always so aware of the
stream of time, notice the quaint clock high on
Massachusetts Hall? Never supplied with clock-
work or a pair of hands, this giant clock helps time
to stand forever still in Harvard's ancient yard.

The many-paned windows of these colonial
buildings beamed their welcome to Thoreau. If

in his shyness Thoreau did not respond as warmly as did other writers before and since, that was the fault of Thoreau rather than of Harvard. Ralph Waldo Emerson, Oliver Wendell Holmes, Henry Wadsworth Longfellow, and James Russell Lowell loved this spot. Perhaps, in his quiet way, Henry Thoreau also admired his university. If so, we lack the proof.

Many willing hands helped Thoreau through

college. He himself earned what he could, making pencils and picking berries during his summer vacations. His father added a few dollars. So did his admiring aunts and his sister Helen who was now teaching school. Harvard granted a small scholarship. Even so, Henry Thoreau needed to live simply. He ate at a commons table for $1.35 a week and shared a room in Hollis Hall. By necessity he wore his green homespun coat to chapel instead of the usual black. This caused talk among the boys.

He did not have the extra money to join the other young men in noisy oyster suppers. But if some of the wilder students thought that Thoreau was "getting little out of Harvard," they did not know what was going on inside his head. While they were setting off small explosions and otherwise running riot, Thoreau was enjoying rarer adventures. His pleasures were largely of the mind.

At Harvard, Thoreau mastered Greek and Latin which he read for sheer pleasure. He studied mathematics and wrote many English themes. He also learned some Spanish, French, Italian, and German. Most of these studies were useful to him in later life.

Although he was never at the top of his class, Thoreau was usually in the upper third, a good student if not a brilliant one. Actually his mind was often elsewhere — still sighing for the woods and waters of his native Concord, or soaring to far countries where he hoped he might someday travel. Boats and books fascinated Thoreau. Both could transport one to distant lands.

Southward from Cambridge lies the great city of Boston. Thoreau hated all cities, including this nearby port across the Charles River. But he was in love with the wharves along the Boston waterfront.

Here his father's father, John Thoreau, had made his small fortune. This first Thoreau in America had left the Isle of Jersey in the year 1773 and had crossed the Atlantic to try his luck in Boston. During the Revolution he had sailed as a privateer. After the war he began as a merchant, with a single barrel of sugar for capital. This he finally increased to the tidy sum of $25,000.

Little of grandfather's money now remained in the family. But Henry liked to visit the wharves and think of the many Thoreaus who had thrived by ocean commerce. He believed that much farther back his ancestors may have been bold Vikings, rowing their dragon-prowed vessels through stormy seas.

The waterfront odors of codfish, tar, and hemp, mingling with spices from the Orient, produced a sharp fragrance which Thoreau enjoyed. He would stand for hours watching the weather-beaten fishing boats unloading their catch, or swift packets of the China trade booming up the harbor under a cloud of sail. Here too were ships loading thousands of tons of Massachusetts ice for customers as far away as India.

It takes money to travel by boat. It takes much

less to travel by book. As the poet Emily Dickinson wrote:

> There is no frigate like a book
> To take us lands away . . .

Open the pages of a book and snowy sails are spread to the wind; waves curl toward the horizon. Where else may the reader have for a traveling companion —

Brave Ulysses returning from the Trojan War!

Christopher Columbus in search of a westward
passage to India!

Marco Polo bound for far Cathay!

Time and space are no barrier in a book. The
printed page is a magic carpet. Even a poor boy
like Thoreau could travel anywhere he wished.
No wonder he liked the Harvard Library.

Fellow students noticed that Thoreau usually
walked with his eyes cast down, thinking his own
thoughts, striding like an Indian toward University Hall. Only later did they realize that he
was seeing much more than some who were
looking straight ahead.

Once during these years Thoreau went camping
with a friend. He was allowed a leave of absence
to teach school. Illness made his return as a senior
difficult. But the greatest event during Thoreau's
Harvard career was his discovery of an inspiring
little volume by Emerson entitled *Nature*.

Ralph Waldo Emerson was descended from a
long line of New England preachers. He too was
a Harvard man, having graduated twelve years
before Thoreau entered as a freshman. Emerson

had given up preaching to become a writer and lecturer. Now, after a long absence, he had returned to Concord where he would write his books and rear his children.

Although they were not yet friends, Emerson and Thoreau were aware of each other. Emerson had written a letter to the President of Harvard which helped Thoreau to retain his scholarship during his senior year. And Thoreau was now reading Emerson's *Nature,* a book sparkling with new ideas.

Emerson was brave and hopeful.

He was interested in the entire universe.

He believed young men should build their own world.

Emerson's book lit a lively bonfire in Thoreau's brain. In his graduation address in August, 1837, Thoreau surprised his audience by suggesting that everyone should labor only one day a week and spend the other six enjoying the "sublime revelations of nature."

Such a program would not have worked then, and it will not work now! On this schedule most of the world would starve. Thoreau, however, tried at times to live by this strange calendar, and in so doing made himself poor, while enriching the world. Many still see nature through the eyes of Henry David Thoreau who had the courage to spend most of his life recording the opening of every flower and the return of every bird.

Henry Thoreau graduated from Harvard with good grades. But he refused to pay a small fee for his sheepskin diploma. He later said that he believed every sheep should keep its own skin.

Home from Harvard, Thoreau wrote a poem or two, walked in the woods and drifted on the river playing his flute. Soon he must decide how he would earn his living. But for the moment he was enjoying his homecoming.

He had not studied law, medicine, or religion. Therefore he could not be a lawyer, a doctor, or a preacher. He could always teach school. But here too there was a difficulty. In those days the "three R's" — Reading and 'Riting and 'Rithmetic — were "taught to the tune of a hickory stick." In

fact it sometimes seemed that schoolmasters spent
more time beating children than instructing them.
Thoreau, however, thought such methods were
stupid. He did not believe in whipping pupils.

To an older friend he wrote, "I could make
education a pleasant thing both to the teacher and
the scholar.... We should seek to be fellow-
students with the pupil."

In that first autumn after his graduation,
Thoreau became the teacher of the Concord
"town school" — serving for the shortest term on
record. He announced that he would not whip
the students, but would "talk morals" instead.

Within two weeks a member of the school committee visited the classroom. This grim deacon
told Thoreau that he must beat the children or
the school "would spoil." Thoreau, thoroughly
angry, seized the first six pupils at hand and gave
each a few sharp raps. Then he quit his job,
telling the deacon that he and his committee could
run the school to suit themselves.

Some neighbors were amused; some annoyed.
At least one of the pupils thus whipped held a

grudge against Thoreau for the rest of his life. But the village now understood that Henry Thoreau had ideas of his own about school-teaching.

During the remainder of that autumn and the following winter Thoreau looked unsuccessfully for another teaching position. Doubtless his ideas on education were too advanced to please most school authorities of his time. Meanwhile he dreamed of other jobs he might enjoy in far places. He could be "a Greenland whaler, or a settler on the Columbia River, or a Canton merchant, or a soldier in Florida ... or a Robinson Crusoe in the Pacific or a silent navigator of any sea. So wide is the choice ..."

Unable to find a teaching job with any established school, Thoreau started an academy of his own in Concord. By the next autumn Henry and his brother John were successfully operating this private school where they could follow their own plans for teaching. Soon they had twenty-five scholars and a waiting list and had moved into the old Concord Academy (where Thoreau had been prepared for Harvard).

Henry taught Latin, Greek, French, and higher mathematics. John taught other subjects and was the principal. The children "loved John and respected Henry." And although the pupils were not whipped, they nevertheless behaved remarkably well. They enjoyed the school and learned rapidly.

One of the most attractive boys studying at this new academy was Edmund Sewall, a nephew of Miss Prudence Ward who roomed and boarded with the Thoreaus. In a letter written at about this time, Edmund speaks of the pleasures of being a pupil of Henry Thoreau:

> I am going to school in Concord to a Mr. Thoreau, who is a very pleasant schoolmaster. Saturdays we do nothing but write compositions. I have been out to sail once in Mr. Thoreau's boat. He has a very good boat, which he and his brother built themselves. The river was high, and we sailed very fast a part of the way.

Not only Edmund Sewall, but many of the

other students were given boat trips on the river. The boys were also taken swimming, and the whole class went on nature walks.

Today such "progressive" methods are used in many schools. But in the 1830's these reforms seemed radical indeed. No whipping! Happy jaunts and picnics along the river! Obviously such a school "would spoil."

Far from "spoiling," the new Concord Academy became one of the most successful schools in the whole region. Each week the students were taken on a walk, or a boat trip with side excursions on the shore. Henry Thoreau was particularly successful in teaching his pupils about the Indians who in earlier days had lived along these waters.

Thoreau would bring the boat to the shore at a place where he thought the Indians might once have lived. Moving up the bank he would say: "Do you see anything here that would be likely to attract Indians to this spot?"

One boy would suggest that here was good fishing. Another pointed to the woods where the Indians could hunt. A third boy noticed a clear little stream from which they could drink. Still another concluded that the hillside would protect the wigwams from the bitter north wind.

As the biographer Sanborn tells the story, Thoreau then took his spade and began striking it into the soft earth. Finally he hit a stone. Removing the turf, he found just what he was seeking — a circle of blackened hearthstones where the

Indians had had their fireplace.

Thoreau usually could find for the boys an Indian arrowhead, as sharp as the day the arrow maker had chipped the flint into a useful point. As Thoreau told his class of those dusky warriors, the boys could virtually see them skimming over Concord water in their birch-bark canoes.

No wonder more and more pupils came to the Concord Academy. For the moment, it seemed that Henry Thoreau had found his calling and would make a success of his interesting profession.

Ralph Waldo Emerson was a bright and gentle person who always attracted friends. He and his wife Lidian had a comfortable home in Concord which was the gathering place of thinkers and writers.

To the Emerson house came such people as Bronson Alcott, the philosopher; Margaret Fuller, the champion of women's rights; Jones Very, the half-mad poet, and other strange and interesting people. Of this group Henry Thoreau was the youngest.

Not long out of Harvard, with vague ambitions and unpolished manners, Thoreau could be difficult. He liked to say No when other people said Yes. There was an air of wildness about him like that of a caged hawk. He had flashing gray-blue eyes. His nose was long and his speech had a burr that was almost Scotch. He so greatly admired Emerson that he seemed to be trying to look like him. But sometimes he was rude even to Emerson.

Thoreau, who was gentle with children and with animals, sparked and crackled when arguing with his adult friends.

What did these people talk about? Everything under the sun:

Freeing the slaves in the South.

Improving schools.

Equal rights for women.

Better working conditions for laborers.

Poetry, history, religion.

Hindu philosophy.

In brief, anything that was exciting — new or old.

They believed in "plain living and high thinking." Some people called them "Transcendentalists" since in their conversation and writing they *transcended*, or rose above, everyday thoughts.

One had to be intelligent and well informed to keep up with the conversation at Emerson's house. And it was well to be interested in reforming mankind and bettering the world.

Perhaps one reason why Thoreau argued sharply with these reformers was because he was not particularly concerned about improving other people. He thought that the best way to better the world was first to improve yourself.

An excellent way to improve yourself is to keep a journal — writing down each day what you do, the thoughts you think, and the books you read. Emerson suggested that Thoreau start a journal, and Henry began immediately and continued faithfully throughout his life.

It is in Thoreau's wonderful journals that we find his thoughtful reports on nature in the Concord region from October, 1837, to November, 1861. His reward for all this work? It was never in cash. He took his pay in sunrises and sunsets, in the fragrance of flowers and the songs of birds. You cannot cash moonbeams at the bank: they are a very "transcendental" form of money. But that was the kind of money that Thoreau preferred.

Years later, if anyone had asked Thoreau what he had done during his life, he might proudly have answered, "I kept a journal."

A Week on the Concord and Merrimack Rivers

3

ALL OF THE MEN in the Thoreau family were good craftsmen, clever with tools. It is not surprising, therefore, that the boat which Henry and John had built in the spring of 1839 "sailed very fast."

It was shaped like a fisherman's dory, fifteen feet long by three and one-half feet wide. It was painted green below to match the water with a border of blue above to match the sky. It had two masts, one of which could be taken out to serve as a tent pole at night, and it was equipped with two sets of oars.

Henry believed that a boat should be half fish
and half bird — slipping through the water like
a fish, with sails like the wings of a gull. The boys
were quite justifiably proud of this fine boat. They
named it the *Musketaquid,* meaning Meadow
River, the old Indian name for the Concord.

The month of May came with its blossoming
orchards, and June with its water lilies. Then
came July, and Ellen Sewall, a lively girl of seven-
teen. She was the sister of Edmund Sewall, the
boy at the Concord Academy. Her aunt, Miss
Prudence Ward, had invited Ellen to Concord to
be her guest at the Thoreaus'.

Both young men promptly fell in love with this
summer visitor. Each took her sailing in the boat.
Henry disliked circus parades, but he gladly took
Ellen to see a giraffe that was being exhibited by
a traveling show. John was as enamored as Henry.
Ellen's visit seemed much too short. The Thoreau
brothers wished she might stay for months.

Henry and John had planned for their vacation,
a boat trip on the Concord and Merrimack Rivers.
Perhaps their preparation for this journey helped

to take their thoughts away from their new and disturbing friend.

Their plan was to sail down the Concord to the Merrimack, then up the Merrimack many miles and return. They had a tent, buffalo robes, and various provisions from their own garden. Because they hoped to live like Indians they took guns and probably fish lines. For pulling the boat around waterfalls they brought a pair of wheels.

Not even Captain Cook could have felt more adventuresome than Henry and John Thoreau on Saturday, August 31, 1839.

A fine rain obscured the misty morning. But the afternoon was clear and mild.

"So with a vigorous shove," wrote Thoreau in his book *A Week on the Concord and Merrimack Rivers*, "we launched our boat from the bank, while the flags and bulrushes curtseyed a God-speed, and dropped silently down the stream."

Some friends waved good-by from a lower point. The boys shot their guns into the air as a happy farewell salute. Soon they were floating past the ruins of the old North Bridge, "the first regular battleground of the Revolution."

"Gradually the village murmur subsided, and we seemed to be embarked on the placid current of our dreams, floating from past to future."

Turtles slipped from their logs as the boat approached. Sometimes a swift pickerel would be startled from its hiding place under a lily pad. Sunfish as bright as jewels flashed through the water.

The Concord here flows between wide, grassy meadows where late summer flowers and masses of willows were reflected in the stream. So calm was this mirror that all their joys seemed double. At last the spire of the village church of Concord was out of sight. Far behind lay home and friends. Ahead lay the Carlisle Bridge under which they soon were passing.

Late in the afternoon they saw a man fishing with "a long birch pole, its silvery bark left on." He brought to mind a whole race of old fishermen who had haunted this river.

After they had rowed seven miles, evening

began to descend. Cowbells tinkled across the darkening pastures.

They moored their boat "on the west side of a little rising ground which in the spring forms an island in the river." Soon they had built a cheerful fire and were cooking their evening meal.

They pitched their tent on the hillside a few rods from the shore and sat looking toward the sunset where pine trees lifted "plumes against the sky." They lay awake for a while listening to the "breathing of the wind," the cry of an owl, and the drowsy twittering of a few birds. Once they heard a muskrat "fumbling among the potatoes and melons" in their boat, but when they hurried through the dusk to chase this robber away, they could see only a ripple in the water where he had plunged to safety. Several times they heard "foxes stepping about over the dead leaves, and brushing the dewy grass" close to the tent.

Once during the night they were awakened by the distant alarm bells. Far away on the horizon above the town of Lowell they saw such light that

they knew there must be a fire. Then they slept again until dawn.

This morning being Sunday, they glided through a rosy mist on the wide, dark river, hearing church bells from village steeples. So still was the surface that "a kingfisher or robin over the river was as distinctly seen reflected in the water below as in the air above." Every oak and birch and elm and willow on the shore was likewise mirrored. Even the frogs seemed to be meditating Sabbath thoughts.

Both boys may have been thinking of Ellen Sewall on this Sunday morning. Henry certainly was, for he wrote in his book: "On this same stream a maiden once sailed in my boat . . . and as she sat in the prow there was nothing but herself between the steersman and the sky."

At last, reaching the falls of the Concord, they could go no farther down this river, but must turn left into the Middlesex canal. This man-made waterway allowed canal boats a short cut from Boston Harbor to the Merrimack River. The Thoreaus, using part of this cut-across, made six miles in a single hour, taking turns on the tow-path pulling the boat. They reached the Merrimack just above Pawtucket Falls where a friendly lockkeeper left his book to let them through the locks and down into the river.

They found the Merrimack an active and lively stream, very different from the slow-moving Concord down which they had drifted. Here they were fighting their way upstream against the current. So now they must bend to their oars.

Henry Thoreau would one day trace the Merrimack from its crystal springs high in the White Mountains to its mouth on the Atlantic coast. But on this first day of September in 1839 he was testing its currents for the first time. The good ship *Musketaquid* behaved very well in this swift water.

As they rowed upstream Henry and John talked of the Indians who not so many generations before had fought and fished and feasted on these shores. Many an arrow and bullet had found its mark along this stream. In the old cemeteries lay the bones of pioneers who had died fighting the Indians.

Wildest of all the true stories of those bloody times was that of Hannah Dustin captured by the Indians. "She had seen her seven elder children flee with their father, but knew not of their fate." She had seen her baby murdered "and had left her own and her neighbors' dwellings in ashes. When she reached the wigwam of her captor, situated on an island in the Merrimack . . . she had been told that she and her nurse were soon to be taken to a distant Indian settlement, and there made to run the gauntlet..."

But Hannah Dustin, gentle wife and mother though she had always been, decided differently. "She arose before daybreak... and taking the Indians' tomahawks... killed them all in their sleep, excepting one favorite boy..."

Then she and the two other captives — her nurse and an English boy — "collected all the provision they could find," took their dead captor's gun, and "scuttling all the canoes but one," began their flight homeward down sixty rushing miles of the river. When the two tired women and the boy reached home they had proof of their wild adventure — the scalps of several Indians.

No longer were there red men lurking behind each rock and pine along the shore. But Henry and John Thoreau, telling each other such stories as they pulled against the stream, increased the excitement of their voyage.

On Monday, Tuesday, and Wednesday they continued up and up the Merrimack. Today on

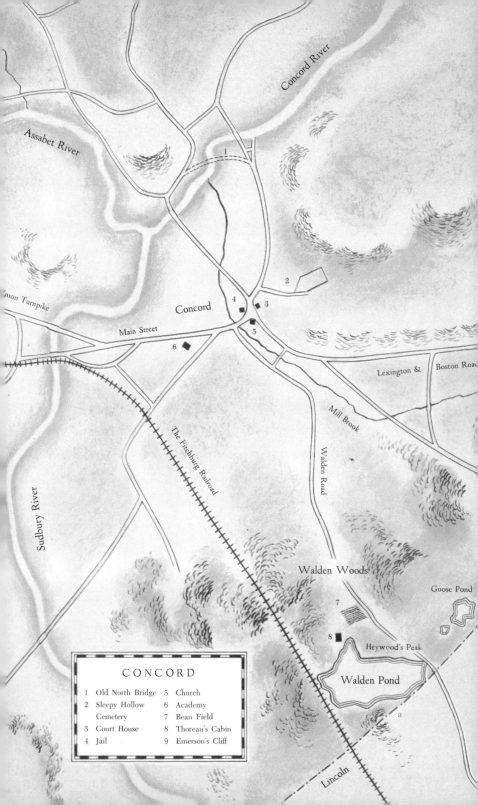

Assabet River

Concord River

Union Turnpike

Concord

Main Street

Lexington & Boston Road

Mill Brook

The Fitchburg Railroad

Walden Road

Sudbury River

Walden Woods

Goose Pond

Heywood's Peak

Walden Pond

Lincoln

1
2
3
4
5
6
7
8
9

CONCORD

1 Old North Bridge
2 Sleepy Hollow
  Cemetery
3 Court House
4 Jail

5 Church
6 Academy
7 Bean Field
8 Thoreau's Cabin
9 Emerson's Cliff

most maps it is hard to find the names of the rapids and waterfalls that blocked their path, but each was a fresh experience to the Thoreaus. At every waterfall they floated their boat into the locks, to be lifted by the power of rising water to the river level above. Most impressive of all the cascades was the great Amoskeag Falls at Manchester, already turning water wheels in 1839.

Once they watched piles of logs being tumbled from a cliff into the river to be floated downstream to some sawmill. Often they saw canal boats loaded with thousands of bricks, piles of cordwood, or other products, gliding down the river to markets nearer the ocean.

In earlier years, Henry and John had envied these carefree boatmen. Now, in their twenties, they envied them still. In the front of one boat they saw "a brawny New Hampshire man, leaning on his pole, bareheaded and in shirt and trousers only, a rude Apollo of a man, coming down from that 'vast uplandish country' . . . of nameless age, with flaxen hair," vigorous and weather-beaten of countenance.

Obviously the boys were enjoying their trip. Rowing their boat along, swimming from sand bars, resting under the forest trees, getting provisions from lockkeepers, the two brothers worked farther and farther up this clear, fast stream, seeing now and then the flash of pickerel or trout.

At last, when they were tired of rowing, they left their boat securely tied, and began a full week's excursion overland. By foot and by stagecoach they went to Franconia Notch where they viewed The Great Stone Face known also as the Old Man of the Mountain. Then, after scaling the summit of Mount Washington, they made their return to the boat, finding it untouched and with all their provisions and belongings just as they had left them.

They fairly raced downstream on Thursday. That night the weather changed. "We had gone to bed in summer, and we awoke in autumn." As they swept down the swift current on Friday morning, the sumac and maple were already touched by frost. Crimson and gold began to appear in the green of the forest. "Cattle were heard to low wildly in the pastures and along the highways . . ." as though in fear of coming winter. The cottages of farmers and lockkeepers looked cozier, promising warmth for the bitter months to come.

Running downstream ahead of a stiff breeze, the *Musketaquid* now seemed to fly, like the half bird it was, through a valley where asters and goldenrod gleamed and where orchards were heavy with ripe fruit. Swept by gusts of autumn wind, the river helped to speed the boat — down, down the lovely Merrimack.

The same quiet lockkeeper took them into the canal. Soon they were rowing through a more gentle evening, from which the wind had fallen away, up the silent, slow-flowing Concord River. Two great blue herons drifted across the sky. A few stars came out. All was peace and solitude with only the dip of the oars to break the silence.

Wrote Thoreau, "We had made about fifty miles this day with sail and oar, and now, far in the evening, our boat was grating against the bulrushes of its native port . . . we leaped gladly on

shore, drawing it up, and fastening it to the wild apple tree, whose stem still bore the mark which its chain had worn in the chafing of the spring freshets."

The town seemed empty that autumn without Ellen Sewall. Both John and Henry were restless thinking of this attractive girl. First one and then the other visited her at her home in the town of Scituate on the Atlantic shore. John sent her opals for her collection of stones. Henry wrote sad and lofty poems which were meant to show his love. Letters flew back and forth from Concord to Scituate.

Both boys were in love with Ellen. But whom did Ellen love?

Summer again came to Concord, and Ellen once more visited the Thoreaus. Family tradition later insisted that Henry stepped nobly aside to let John propose marriage.

In a moment of impulse Ellen accepted John's proposal. Later she changed her mind, partly because her parents objected. Suddenly Henry was free to ask for Ellen's hand himself. At this point his journal shows a leap from sadness to utmost joy.

But Henry Thoreau, who could talk freely enough with his mother and his aunts, was never at ease with pretty young girls. In a letter written late in the bleak autumn of 1840 he asked Ellen to marry him. But his proposal was probably both shy and vague — as strange as some of those poems he had written. She hated to hurt him, but her answer was No.

In a letter to her Aunt Prudence Ward, Ellen confessed, "I never felt so badly at sending a letter in my life." She could not "bear to think that both these friends" whom she had "enjoyed so much" would no longer be her companions in Concord and Scituate.

Both young men had tried and failed. Ellen married another and raised a fine family. But the two youthful schoolteachers were not happy that semester.

In the spring of 1841 the students of the Concord Academy were surprised to learn that the

school would soon close its doors. It had been a
a thriving and successful academy, but it was
now going out of business. John Thoreau was not
well — probably his first touch of the family
tendency toward tuberculosis. Without John's
steady hand as principal of the school, Henry's
interest in the project quickly waned.

Less than a year later, in January, 1842, John
Thoreau injured his wrist on a rusty nail. Lockjaw
quickly set in, and he died in great pain, brave and
charming to the end. Henry, who had shared a
room with John since they were little boys, suffered almost as much as John as he lay dying.

When Henry later published the record of their
trip together — *A Week on the Concord and
Merrimack Rivers* — he began it with a verse
meant for John:

> Where'er thou sail'st who sailed with me,
> Though now thou climbest loftier mounts
> And fairer rivers dost ascend,
> Be thou my Muse, my Brother —

And the *Musketaquid* — the sailboat they had

built so happily together? Thoreau could not see it without thinking of John and Ellen — two friends he had lost forever. He sold it to a young writer named Nathaniel Hawthorne who had just moved to Concord. And Hawthorne's happy bride, Sophia, renamed it the *Pond Lily.*

Handy Man and Private Tutor

4

AFTER THE Concord Academy closed its doors, Henry Thoreau seemed the "only man of leisure" in the village. Those who knew him best, however, realized that he was seldom idle.

He was a jack-of-all-trades and master of several. He could build a fence or a boat or a house. He was a good gardener and knew how to prune a grapevine or a fruit tree. He could milk a cow, harness and drive a team of horses. He was an excellent surveyor. The pencils he made were among the best manufactured in America.

"A noble, manly youth," said Emerson, "a scholar and poet and as full of buds of promise as a young apple tree."

Emerson, the busy lecturer and writer, needed a handy man and caretaker to tend his orchard and his garden, make minor repairs around the place, and do the hundreds of other chores for which he himself had neither the talent nor the time. The Emerson children needed an outdoor companion wise in the ways of nature.

When Emerson was away on lecture trips it would be comforting to know that he was leaving his house and grounds in the hands of a trustworthy and industrious friend, ready to do the bidding of his wife Lidian who had a tendency to be "pensive . . . and melancholy."

Emerson suggested that Henry come to live with them. He was to have the little front room at the head of the stairs, his board, and such leisure as he needed to roam the woods and to write in his journal. He was to do only such labor as he himself chose to do.

It is true that Emerson was being generous and thoughtful in offering his young friend this opportunity. But it was not sheer charity as some have suggested. Try today, if you will, to find a

Harvard-trained handy man willing to work without pay for room and board only.

What made this offer almost irresistible to Thoreau was the fact that the Emerson house was the center of all the intellectual life in Concord. Emerson attracted bright minds and soaring spirits as a candle attracts moths.

Margaret Fuller, the lively young woman of advanced ideas, often came as a visitor to Concord, staying at the Emerson house. Just now, with Emerson's backing, she was editing a little magazine called *The Dial* where Thoreau's first published poem appeared.

Bronson Alcott, the gentle and not very practical philosopher, had moved to Concord with his brave, penniless family. This very talkative and saintly-looking man with his long fair hair and bright blue eyes was often to be found in Emerson's parlor solving the problems of the universe.

Another new arrival was the dark and handsome Nathaniel Hawthorne who would later become famous as the author of *The Scarlet Letter* and *The House of Seven Gables*. He and his bride

Sophia were living very happily in the Old Manse where the late Dr. Ripley and Emerson himself had at one time lived.

Emerson asked Thoreau to help the newly arrived Hawthornes prepare the garden at the Old Manse. Hawthorne found this handy man an interesting and unusual human being.

"He is . . . a young man with much of wild, original nature still remaining in him," Hawthorne

recorded. He noticed Henry's "somewhat rustic, although courteous manners ..." and was surprised to learn that Thoreau "repudiated all regular modes of getting a living, and seems inclined to lead a sort of Indian life."

"A keen and delicate observer of nature," Hawthorne wrote of his new friend, "and nature, in return for his love, seems to adopt him as her especial child, and shows him secrets which few others are allowed to witness. He is familiar with beast, fish, fowl, and reptile, and has strange stories to tell ..."

Thoreau taught Hawthorne how to row and sail the boat which he had sold him. When winter came, these two and Emerson went skating. Thoreau was seen leaping and cutting figures on the ice, Hawthorne moving gravely like a "Greek statue" in his long cloak, and Emerson "too weary to hold himself erect, pitching head foremost, half lying on the air."

Poor Emerson! He was much older than his two companions, but spirited as always when anyone proposed rowing, skating, or a berry-picking party. Henry Thoreau led him a lively pace.

Emerson had invited Thoreau to stay for twelve months. Two years after that invitation was issued, the young writer was still living in the little room at the head of the stairs, doing the odd jobs, helping to edit *The Dial,* and adding his very sharp comments at the gatherings of Transcendentalists in the parlor. For Thoreau's sake, and perhaps for his own, the gentle, generous Emerson believed it was time for a change.

On May 1, 1843, Thoreau left Concord for New York City. He would soon be twenty-six years of age, and his ambition was to become a lecturer and an author.

Most young men and women coming to New York to seek their fortune are thrilled by the big town. But Henry David Thoreau, who would always be a village boy at heart, distrusted cities. True, a job awaited him; and in his pocket were letters of introduction to several famous men, including the newspaper publisher Horace

Greeley. But Thoreau was on his guard as his ship sailed up to a wharf "just the other side of their Castle Garden."

From this vantage point at the foot of the Battery, Thoreau would have been able to see a forest of masts, smart packets arriving from Europe, and busy side-wheelers shuttling up and down the Hudson and the East River. He was viewing one of the greatest ports in the world, a city of more than 300,000 which offered him the challenge of success or failure. But his comment was defensive: "I do not like their cities and forts, with their morning and evening guns . . . I want a whole continent to breathe in, and a good deal of solitude and silence, such as Wall Street cannot buy — nor Broadway with its wooden pavement."

Thoreau's job was an easy one. Emerson had arranged with his brother William, who lived on Staten Island, to hire Thoreau as a part-time tutor for William's son, Haven. Thoreau was to have a room of his own, his meals, a small salary, and leisure time to meet the editors and book publishers of New York with the hope that he might interest them in his writing. New York City, then as now, was but a short ferry ride across the harbor.

From his homesick letters, however, no reader would have gathered that Thoreau appreciated this opportunity. It is true that he visited many editors, but without much success. He tried vainly to interest the book publishing firm of Harpers. "They say they are making $50,000 annually, and their motto is to let well alone."

New York City in those days was noisy and rough enough to dismay any country boy. One needed "a pair of eyes in the back of the neck" to avoid being run over by the roaring traffic of horse-drawn hackneys, private coaches, and omnibuses. Along three miles of Broadway the promenading women, dressed in the French fashion, were "a moving bed of tulips." But shy Henry Thoreau preferred the quieter women of Concord and wrote tenderly to his mother and to Emerson's wife, Lidian, whom he held in the affectionate regard of an older sister.

"Am I not made of Concord dust?" he asked. Shutting his eyes he could easily believe that he was back in his native village and not on the shores of Staten Island. "I cannot realize that it is the roar of the sea I hear now, and not the wind in Walden woods."

He wanted "solitude and silence." Instead he saw a city which, by gaslight, in such areas as Five Points was unsafe for respectable citizens. "Gangs of hardened wretches" roamed many of the streets. The volunteer firemen who rushed to every blaze were almost as tough as the ruffians who reeled from the hundreds of grogshops. Epidemics of yellow fever and cholera regularly swept the city. And ferocious pigs fed on the garbage thrown into the littered alleys.

Thoreau in a bitter letter to Emerson said, "The pigs in the street are the most respectable part of the population."

True there were art galleries, Barnum's Museum, theaters, luxurious hotels such as the Astor House, and beautiful private homes. But Thoreau, who had little money, saw mostly the meaner aspects of the city, the broken pavements, the streets and wharves littered with boxes and bales, and the great, restless crowds. The poet Walt Whitman, whom Thoreau would one day meet, loved all this bustle and noise. The cries of the street vendors were music to Whitman's ears. Thoreau, however, longed for village sounds and the "wind in Walden Woods."

Horace Greeley, publisher of the *Tribune*, tried to aid Thoreau. He offered to help him sell his articles — an act of pure generosity. However he also offered fatherly advice, "Now be neighborly!"

This was an excellent suggestion, but hard for Henry to follow. Much as he loved his own family and certain other human beings, Thoreau could not admire the mass of mankind. He found New York crowds "a thousand times meaner than I could have imagined." He wondered when the world would realize the importance and dignity of the individual.

The two things Thoreau enjoyed in New York were those he had enjoyed in Cambridge and

Boston — boats and books:

"From an old ruined fort on Staten Island" he would watch some vessel from the moment "when she first came upon the coast, and her hull heaved up and glistened in the sun," until that later hour when the "most adventurous news-boat met her" and she moved "past the Hook, and up the narrow channel of the wide bay. . . ."

He liked seagoing craft of every design and

description, "the long procession of vessels getting to sea . . . far as the eye could reach . . . ships, barks, brigs, schooners and sloops."

Such days Thoreau relished as he did those spent in various New York libraries. He continued to be a serious student with an active and eager mind.

Generally speaking, however, Thoreau was unhappy in New York. He managed to publish a few pages of his writing, but earned so little from this that it would scarcely have kept a sparrow alive. He seems to have made virtually no friends except Horace Greeley. He wrote, "I walked through New York yesterday — and met no real and living person."

In an affectionate letter to his family he said, "My thoughts revert to those dear hills and that *river* which fills up the world to its brim . . . staying at home is the heavenly way."

Anyone who has ever celebrated Thanksgiving in New England — the frosty air, the maples like blue woodsmoke against the horizon, the fields rich with corn shocks and golden pumpkins, the roast turkey and stuffing sending their spicy fragrance through the house — all who remember these old-fashioned Thanksgivings will realize why Thoreau in late November could no longer endure New York. So once again he packed his bag with his books and few belongings. He arrived safely in Concord in time for Thanksgiving.

Walden Pond

5

THOREAU HAD always loved Walden. Having returned to Concord, he now planned a cottage on its shore.

"Near the end of March, 1845, I borrowed an axe and went down to the woods by Walden Pond . . . and began to cut down some tall, arrowy white pines, still in their youth, for timber . . . It was a pleasant hillside where I worked, covered with pine woods, through which I looked out on the pond. . . ."

Soon rain was melting the last ice. Thoreau heard a lark, then a stray wild goose groping through the mist "like the spirit of the fog."

It takes "a little Yankee shrewdness" to build a

home. But if foxes have holes and birds of the air have nests, surely man can build himself a shelter with but little greater labor.

"I hewed the main timbers six inches square," says Thoreau, who was a good carpenter. These he mortised securely at each joint. "I usually carried my dinner of bread and butter, and read the newspaper in which it was wrapped, at noon, sitting amid the green pine boughs." Everything was scented with the fragrance of pine.

Where a woodchuck once had tunneled, Thoreau dug his cellar in the sandy soil. In May some friends came to help him set up the framework, making a picnic of the occasion. To this framework Thoreau nailed boards he had purchased at a bargain. Soon he had a neat cabin ten feet wide and fifteen feet long with "a garret and a closet, a large window on each side." There was a door at one end of the house, and a fireplace (soon to be built) at the other. All this he acquired at a total cost of $28.12½ plus several weeks of enjoyable labor.

Thoreau had always desired a hideaway of his

own. Now he could live undisturbed and write his books. He wanted no curtains at his windows to shut out the sunlight and moonlight. He wanted no rug upon his floor to cover the clean pine boards. He made (or borrowed from Concord attics) his few pieces of furniture.

He had cooking and eating utensils, plus a spade and a wheelbarrow. On his desk he kept a few books, writing paper, and an oil lamp. He never locked his door.

"Simplify, simplify, simplify" was his motto.

Food was no great problem: fish from the lake, wild berries from the woods, vegetables from his garden, rice and hoecakes! It cost him about 27 cents a week for groceries. (One must remember, however, that money in those days would purchase eight or ten times what it will today.)

His cabin was not yet plastered. Nevertheless on July 4, Thoreau moved into his new dwelling. "The upright white hewn studs and freshly planed door and window casings gave it a clean and airy look, especially in the morning, when its timbers were saturated with dew." The morning sun rose clear. The morning wind came through the chinks in the unplastered wall. Thoreau was up with the dawn for his dip in Walden Pond.

Why did Thoreau go to the woods, and how did he live there? As we have seen, he hated the city. He loved silence and solitude. He wanted to be alone with the seasons; to live something like a woodchuck or a fox. He wanted to know what makes the universe tick, and why man is part of that universe.

Thoreau felt lonely in the crowds of New York City. But he never felt lonely when he was by himself at Walden. All around him he heard the rustling and bustling of nature. Squirrels chattered; blue jays scolded. How could he feel lonely when he had for company the friendly stars which spangle the midnight sky, the warm moon rising through the Walden pines to pave a path across the pond? Sometimes in the evening he would play his flute. For accompaniment he had the flute's own echoes from the surrounding hills.

Thoreau liked a "broad margin" to his life. He

wanted to improve each moment by enjoying it richly and fully.

He believed that luxuries are often a burden, and that most men devote their lives to laboring frantically for things they do not need.

However, it must not be thought that Thoreau was lazy. Quite the contrary. Anyone who walked or talked with him soon discovered that he had an active body and an active mind. Those two years at Walden were not without accomplishment. Here are some of the things he did:

He built his excellent little house.

He planted a field of beans (of which, more later!).

He fished, picked berries, and cooked his own food.

He cleaned his cabin frequently, taking all of his furniture outdoors so that he could scrub his pine floor with sand and water.

He cut and carried his own firewood (it warmed him twice, first when he split it and later when he burned it).

He read books in several languages, and thought seriously about his reading.

He reported carefully in his journal on owls and woodchucks, wild ducks and muskrats, wood mice and chickadees — in fact every bird, animal, flower, or tree that he thought interesting.

Finally, he labored faithfully on the manuscripts of two books he was writing.

Because he worked efficiently when he was working, Thoreau had time to sit in his doorway in the sun; "to keep an appointment with a beech tree"; to let nature soak into his pores.

It was a pleasant life, but it was not a pointless one. He was living deeply and with a gentle rhythm. He saw no reason for the haste and waste, the hurry and the competition which he had seen in New York. He was not trying to keep up with the Joneses, even in Concord.

"This was sheer idleness to my fellow-townsmen," Thoreau realized, "but if the birds and flowers had tried me by their standard, I should not have been found wanting."

About a quarter of a mile from Thoreau's little house, near the west end of Walden Pond, ran the Fitchburg Railroad. The wind, playing on the telegraph wires, made sweeter music to Thoreau's ear than any symphony composed by man. He loved, too, the haunting sounds of the locomotive's whistle and bell rushing through the night. When the train had passed, Walden returned to even greater solitude.

Thoreau was not an accomplished musician. But deep inside him was a warm appreciation of nature's music. He enjoyed the whippoorwills, calling plaintively through the dusk, the owls, quavering mournfully, "Oh-o-o-o — that I had never been bor-r-r-n!" At the pond's edge, the bull-frogs rumbled *tr-r-r-oonk, tr-r-r-oonk, tr-r-r-oonk.* Thoreau was soothed by the frequent "roar and pelting" of rainstorms upon his tight roof. Hearing this wild music of the Walden Woods, he some-times felt that he was alone on this planet, the first or the last man in the world.

It is wholesome and pleasant to be alone at least part of the time. No wonder he fell asleep easily and awoke eager for the new day.

Thoreau had three chairs in his little house: "One for solitude, two for friendship, three for society."

When visitors came he usually placed these chairs in his "best room," which was outdoors beneath the pine trees — a room furnished by nature and always well swept by the wind. Some-times a wood chopper came to visit him and they talked slowly and gravely together. Once he fed a "real runaway slave," whom he helped northward toward the Canadian border and freedom.

Bronson Alcott, the philosopher, and Ellery Channing, the Concord poet, were always welcome. So were the boys and girls intent upon berrying or fishing. Thoreau was not equally eager to entertain the men of affairs who came to see him: doctors, lawyers, merchants and the rest. Nor did he welcome "uneasy housekeepers" who in his absence pried into his cupboard and looked to see if his sheets were washed as clean as theirs.

In fact Thoreau was gracious to "all honest pilgrims" who came for the sake of friendship, and not from idle curiosity or with the desire to reform him.

Sometimes it was Thoreau who went a-visiting.

"Every day or two I strolled to the village to hear some of the gossip" which, when taken in small doses, "was really as refreshing in its way as the rustle of leaves and the peeping of frogs."

Thoreau thought people were almost as interesting as his four-footed friends. "In one direction from my house there was a colony of muskrats in the river meadows; under the grove of elms and buttonwoods in the other horizon was a village of busy men, as curious to me as if they had been prairie-dogs. . . ." In fact Thoreau was never as much of a lone wolf as he pretended to be.

Having bathed again in the pond, he would don a clean shirt and walk the mile and a half to Concord to visit friends or family and to buy a few groceries.

Occasionally he was invited to dinner by the Emersons or others. Although "well entertained," he seldom remained the entire evening.

"It was very pleasant . . . to launch myself into the night, especially if it was dark and tempestuous, and set sail from some bright parlor or lecture room, with a bag of rye or Indian meal upon my shoulder, for my snug harbor in the woods. . . ."

Thoreau was like a cat in the dark. Even when his eyes could not guide him, his feet always knew their way. At one place the path ran between two pines which were but 18 inches apart. Yet on the darkest nights he had no trouble slipping between them.

Those who thought that Thoreau had lost his way in life should have seen him at night under the stars. He then seemed the least lost man in all of Concord.

Thoreau had planted a bean field of two and one half acres which required much hoeing to keep down the weeds and grass.

From five A.M. until noon on each early summer day of 1845 Thoreau might be seen, barefooted and moving slowly up one row and down the next, his hoe flashing in the sun as he chopped the weeds, and pulled the fresh, moist soil around his plants. Worms, woodchucks, and cool weather were the enemies of these beans, the woodchucks being the worst, having nibbled a whole quarter acre to the ground.

"I came to love my rows, my beans," Thoreau said. They were honest plants, doing the best they could under difficulties.

Thoreau also loved woodchucks, but during his stay at Walden he killed one of these bean-destroyers — an act for which he was later sorry. He realized that the woodchucks had almost as much right to the beans as he had, and were certainly unaware of any evil-doing.

Thoreau enjoyed the sandy soil between his bare toes. He also enjoyed the serenade of a saucy brown thrasher who from the topmost spray of a birch tree sang gaily, "Drop it, drop it, — cover it up, cover it up, — pull it up, pull it up, pull it up."

Thoreau's hard season's work in the bean field

netted him exactly \$8.71½. But he was not discouraged. He had known the joy of his labor, and the pleasure of "making the earth say beans instead of grass."

The best thing about Thoreau's new home was Walden Pond itself — that ever-changing mirror of the sky, now swept with wind, now smoothed again as by an unseen hand.

Thoreau had always admired this little lake. One of his earliest memories was that of being brought to this beautiful pond by his grandmother when he was a very small boy. In later years he came fishing horned pouts (bullheads). He and a companion on a dark summer night would build a fire near the water's edge and cast in their lines. When, after several happy hours, they had at last caught a good mess of fish, they would throw the burning brands of the fire high over the lake, "like skyrockets, which, coming down into the pond, were quenched with a loud hissing." Then in the darkness, whistling a tune, they would start home for Concord.

Thoreau described Walden as "a clear and deep green well, half a mile long," containing "about sixty-one and a half acres; a perennial spring in the midst of pine and oak woods, without any visible inlet or outlet. . . ."

It is so clear that one can see pickerel, perch and other fish at a depth of twenty-five to thirty feet. And it is so clean that Thoreau used it for his drinking water.

Besides its fish, this pond has other wildlife: bullfrogs, a few turtles, mink, and muskrats. Swallows skim over the water. Wild geese and ducks visit the pond during their migrations.

Often a single loon would utter its wild cry — like the laughter of an insane ghost. Thoreau once played a game which lasted for hours with one of these strange water birds, trying to follow it with his boat. But always the loon came up, laughing at Thoreau, where he least expected it.

Thoreau called Walden "a mirror which no stone can crack, whose quicksilver will never wear off. . . ."

The surface of this mirror reflects every change of the weather and the seasons. On clear days the lake is sometimes blue; on stormy days, a dark slate color. Near the shore the golden sand shines through. Often the water is a mysterious green over the greater depths.

Thoreau saw the flowers of spring and summer reflected in this forest mirror. Then came the russet and crimson of September and October. At last the leaves were scattered by the wind, and the mirror of Walden showed bare branches of oak and aspen, and the dark masses of the evergreens. Gone were the "bright tints of October" and in their place had come "the sombre November colors of the surrounding hills."

Throughout the summer Thoreau had cooked his food on an outdoor fire. His house had remained unplastered. Now, with cold weather setting in, he hurried to build his fireplace and to plaster his house against the autumn breezes.

He purchased bricks for his hearth, and used clean Walden sand in his mortar.

Thoreau was proud of his work, particularly when he lit his first fire and saw the firelight flickering on his walls and ceiling. He found "a couple of old fire dogs to keep the wood from the hearth," and said, "it did me good to see the soot form on the back of the chimney which I had built, and I poked the fire with more right and more satisfaction than usual."

Outdoors the wind moaned through the trees and the owls took up their sad November sere-

nade. Abroad in the darkness were his friends the foxes and the raccoons. The wild geese came lumbering in through the dark, their great wings whispering stormy secrets. It was good to be safe indoors beside the fire, roasting chestnuts and wild apples.

On the twenty-second of December, Thoreau awoke to find that Walden had a crystal roof. He now had a skating rink of more than sixty acres in his front yard. Thoreau liked to lie on the clear ice peering down into the "parlor of the fishes." Air bubbles in the ice looked to him like silver coins. He discovered that each of these bubbles behaves like a small burning glass when the sun shines through it, melting the ice slightly where the light is focused.

Each morning Thoreau cut a hole in the ice to dip up a pail of drinking water. He enjoyed watching the bright chips fly through the frosty air. One day he had a happy thought. Why not measure the depth of Walden? For many days he chipped holes — more than 100 in all. Using a stout cod line weighted with a stone he took careful measurements of the exact depth in every part of the pond. No, it was not "bottomless" as some of the villagers thought! But it was remarkably deep for such a small pond — 102 feet in its deepest spot.

Thoreau had fewer visitors after winter set in. This gave him more time to enjoy the squirrels that came for the corn he put out and for the friendly chickadees and saucy blue jays that came for his crumbs. One of his best friends was a dainty wood mouse that scampered all over him, and was so unafraid that it would even sit in Thoreau's hand while eating.

Now, with the world blanketed deep in snow, the partridges went "budding," taking the only food available, the buds of the bushes and small trees. Sometimes he saw or heard a fox, followed perhaps by hounds baying eagerly and mournfully through Walden woods. Occasionally at night the ice of Walden Pond cracked with a thunderous, rippling roar. But Thoreau loved this "great bed-fellow . . . restless in its bed."

Often he walked eight or ten miles through the deepest snow and would return, chilled but happy. When the bitter wind smote him on one cheek, he followed the advice of the Bible and turned the other cheek. But Thoreau was glad on those days to return to his warm fire. More than ever he looked fondly on his pile of driftwood, old fence rails, and fallen branches. When he wanted a roaring fire he used pitch pine.

Wrote Thoreau, "I weathered some merry snow-storms, and spent some cheerful winter evenings by my fireside, while the snow whirled wildly without."

Each sunrise brought some new and satisfying adventure. "Early in the morning, while all things are crisp with frost, men come with fishing-reels and slender lunch, and let down their fine lines through the snowy field to take pickerel and perch."

Fishing through the ice is a chilly but exciting sport. The fishermen were soon hauling in their handsome prizes.

"Ah, the pickerel of Walden! when I see them lying on the ice ... I am always surprised by their rare beauty. . . . They are not green like the pines, nor gray like the stones, nor blue like the sky; but they have, to my eyes, if possible, yet rarer colors, like flowers and precious stones, as if they were pearls ... or crystals of the Walden water. They, of course, are Walden all over and all through; are themselves small Waldens. . . ."

While Thoreau was living in his house by the

pond, a large crew of men came to harvest ice. Having cut thousands of tons of huge ice cubes, they used horses to haul the ice ashore at the west end of the pond near the railroad track. From this point the ice was shipped to Boston where much of it was loaded on sailing ships to be taken to China, India, and other remote markets. Thoreau thought that these great azure crystals of Walden water bound for distant places must certainly take with them some memory of the sky and woods of Walden. Ice for India! It stirred Thoreau's imagination.

Some thoughts had come to Thoreau from India, by way of the Hindu classic, the Bhagavad-Gita. Eastern philosophers had taught him to be more courageous and more serene. Now the message of Walden was being returned to India as cubes of ice.

Perhaps a few drops of Walden water would soon be mingling with the water of the sacred Ganges River. Such were the dreams of this busy hermit, measuring the depth and meaning of Walden Pond.

Spring came at last. By the first of April, Walden was completely free of ice. Bluebirds, song sparrows, and other messengers of spring sang of the great event. Squirrels raced madly through the trees. Grass began to flame green under the warm sun. Walden, which had been asleep all winter, now was awake again.

Thoreau felt that on a fine spring morning, all life is "pasturing freely." He wondered why on days like this the jailer does not "leave open his prison doors, — why the judge does not dismiss his case." On such a morning "all men's sins are forgiven." Thoreau himself went fishing, "standing on the quaking grass and willow roots, where the muskrats lurk," and catching a good string of fish.

And so the first year at Walden ended, and the season went rolling into high summer.

Thoreau says that his second year in this little house was very much like his first, and apparently it was equally enjoyable. However, after two years and two months at Walden he left the woods "for as good a reason" as he came there. Perhaps

he had "several more lives to live."

He had learned that "life near the bone" is the sweetest; that truth alone endures; that however poor your life may seem, you must meet it and live it. Perhaps if you are out of step with mankind it is because you hear a "different drummer." Cling, however, to what you think is right. Hold to your dreams. You can have your castles in the

air — all that you need to do is build foundations under them.

Thoreau thought that most people are "sound asleep" nearly half the time; that we need only to awake to find life beautiful. "Only that day dawns to which we are awake. . . . The sun is but a morning star."

IT WAS Thoreau's deep desire to give the world the best he had in him. He wanted his words to light up the sky like a comet. He was less interested in money or fame than in reaching mankind with his ideas. But the world was very slow to recognize the genius of Thoreau. Meanwhile he must somehow make his living.

When Thoreau left his hut on Walden Pond and came striding down the path to Concord, he found Emerson planning a lecture tour of England. Emerson's wife was a chronic invalid and the Emerson children still needed a companion. Would Thoreau consider a job as manager of the household while Emerson was in England? His old room at the head of the stairs was waiting.

Emerson was still being generous. But he was, once again, getting his money's worth. Thoreau was an utterly dependable friend, and a very useful helper. Lidian Emerson could trust him, and the Emerson children loved him.

Emerson sailed for England on the *Washington Irving* in October, 1847. He did not return until the next summer. Meanwhile life went on at the Emerson house in Concord. Lidian was often ill. But Thoreau aided her in every way he could. Although a gardener had been hired, Thoreau helped with the planting and pruning of fruit trees. He also assisted Bronson Alcott in building a strange summerhouse which Alcott had designed for the Emerson garden. Thoreau, and the rest of Concord, laughed heartily at this very peculiar shelter.

Thoreau's warm reports to Emerson show him to have been relatively happy during this period. "I have banked up the young trees against the winter and the mice. . . . Lidian and I make very good housekeepers . . . Ellen and Edith and Eddy and Aunty Brown keep up the tragedy and comedy. . . of life as usual."

Ellen, Edith, and Eddy Emerson were about eight, six, and three at this time. They all admired and enjoyed Thoreau who took them skating in winter and boating or berry-picking in summer.

Once Eddy asked him seriously, "Mr. Thoreau, will you be my father?" Thoreau, in reporting this in a letter to Emerson used it as a gentle reminder that Emerson must "come back soon."

Emerson did return in midsummer of 1848. Thoreau then moved to the home of his parents, once again helping his father in the pencil-making business. He earned a few additional dollars surveying farms and village lots. This was particularly pleasant work for Thoreau because he could be a "surveyor" in a double sense, concerned not only with boundary lines, but also with the boundless outdoor world. The farmer might think he owned the farm, but Thoreau came away with the true richness of the place, the memory of some beautiful tree or hillside or meadow brook. In a manner of speaking he was the real owner of all the land he surveyed.

Thoreau's schedule during these years varied but slightly. Usually he arose early, put in the morning at some paid employment, then walked for eight or ten miles in the afternoon, making notes of all he saw. In the evening he copied these notes in more finished form into his journals. By lamplight he also worked on his other writing.

Those who say that "the best of Thoreau is in his journals" usually mean that everything he later wrote went through the journals before finding its way into a lecture, a magazine article, or a book. Writing on the professional level is always hard work. But Thoreau worked harder, struggled longer, and published less than most writers. Sometimes he despaired of ever succeeding.

He had been laboring for years now over two book manuscripts. The first was *A Week on the Concord and Merrimack Rivers,* based on the river trip he had taken with his beloved brother John, now dead. Having slaved so long on this book, he finally felt it was ready for publication. One publisher after another, however, sent back his manuscript. Finally, in desperation, Thoreau had the book published at his own expense.

Although some of the reviews were favorable, this volume did not sell, and Thoreau had to manufacture thousands of pencils to earn the money to pay the publisher.

Thoreau's second and much more important book was *Walden,* one of the masterpieces of American literature. It was based, of course, upon the two years he had spent in his little house beside Walden Pond.

Thoreau read the manuscript of *Walden* to Emerson as they sat beneath an oak tree on the bank of the Concord River. Emerson was as pleased and proud as though he himself had written the book. He had always had faith in Henry Thoreau, and here was proof that he had not been mistaken. Emerson called Thoreau's new work "spicy as flagroot."

The failure of Thoreau's first book delayed publication of the second for many years. But at last a publisher accepted *Walden.* It was brought out in the year 1854 by the well-known firm of Ticknor and Fields of Boston.

Even the sale of this fine book went slowly. The enthusiasm of Emerson and Horace Greeley and several reviewers must have given joy to Thoreau who had waited so long for recognition. But no second edition of the book was published until after Thoreau's death. He had no way of knowing that more than a century later, readers all over the world would be spending happy hours with his enduring classic.

Meanwhile Thoreau went faithfully ahead with his nature observations and his journal. His best friend now was the Concord poet, Ellery Channing, who often accompanied Thoreau on his walks, keeping up a lively conversation. Channing, who would later write a biography of Thoreau, pictures him at about this time as an active and earnest man with whom it was pleasant to walk in the woods:

"In height he was about the average; in his build spare, with limbs that were rather longer than usual ... His features were marked: the nose ... very Roman, like one of the portraits of Caesar ... large overhanging brows above the deepest-set blue eyes that could be seen — blue in certain lights and in others gray; the forehead ... full of concentrated energy and purpose." From his lips came a stream of "unusual and instructive sayings."

To this should be added Emerson's description of Thoreau on his daily pilgrimages into the woods:

"Under his arm he carried an old music-book to press plants; in his pocket his diary and pencil, a spy-glass for birds, microscope, jack-knife and twine." He wore stout shoes, sturdy gray trousers,

and a hat which served a very special second
purpose.

It was inside this hat that Thoreau carried particularly rare and interesting plants and flowers
that he would later identify and add to his collection. This was his "botany box" — useful as one
might wish.

Thoreau had much more under his hat than
mere ferns and flowers, however. He also had an
active and inquiring mind. In the fourteen vol-
umes of his published journals we find daily
evidence of his perceptive brain as it recorded
the passing seasons. He believed that were he to
fall asleep for months or years anywhere in the
Concord region, he would know upon awaking
almost the exact calendar date merely by looking
at the flowers in bud or in bloom around him.

He wrote of April brooks washed clean and
bright, alive with fish running up small channels;
of the keen fragrance of mint beside some spring
where he had stopped to drink; of laurel in bloom,
or a distant view of Mount Monadnock.

The mystery and friendliness of midsummer

moonlight nights lured him abroad.

The oaks and maples, blossoming like great red roses against the hillsides after the first frosts, inspired him to write on autumn colors.

No less than other seasons, he loved winter when the snowflakes drifted down on his rough coat, "perfect little wheels with six spokes. . . . The same law that shapes the earth and the stars shapes the snow-flake. . . . There they lie, like the wreck of chariot wheels after a battle in the skies. Meanwhile the meadow mouse shoves them aside in his gallery, the schoolboy casts them in his snow-ball . . . these glorious spangles, the sweepings of heaven's floor. And they all sing . . . of the mysteries of number six: six, six, six."

If there were an official naturalist for each community (as there should be, and as Emerson once suggested), Henry David Thoreau would never have been without employment.

The Maine Woods

7

WE COMMONLY think of Thoreau as a Concord man who never left home and never wished to. This is not entirely correct.

Whenever he could, he went farther afield. Often he strapped a pack on his back and went exploring among the green hills and white villages of New England. Lecturing and surveying occasionally took him away from home. Once he made a brief excursion to Canada. Late in life he even journeyed as far as Minnesota.

Thoreau was fascinated by mountains and by the sea. Concord had neither. Several times he visited Cape Cod to walk the wind-swept beaches. He loved to stand, looking out over the stormy

Atlantic, where "a man may ... put all America behind him." He found it equally pleasurable to climb Mount Monadnock or some other high hill, sleep in his blanket, and rise to greet the new day from the mountain top.

Thoreau said he had "travelled widely" in Concord. Usually he was satisfied with the local woods and meadows which he knew as well as the palm of his hand.

Occasionally, however, he longed for "wilder wildness." He mourned the fact that the "nobler animals" were long since gone from Concord. Never in Thoreau's time could one see in Walden woods "the cougar, panther, lynx, wolverene, wolf, bear, moose, deer, beaver. ..."

The nearest wilderness where these might still be seen was deep in Maine — a region known principally to Indians, wood choppers, and a few hunters and fishermen. Thoreau often dreamed of those vast, dark forests, rushing rivers, and placid lakes where the moose waded and the deer came down to drink.

Three times during his life — in the years 1846,

1853, and 1857 — Thoreau made pilgrimages to the Maine woods. These were among the happiest experiences of his life.

On his first trip he had five companions, including the experienced Maine guide and boatman, "Uncle George" McCauslin. Thoreau and his party worked their way up the West Branch of the Penobscot River in a thirty-foot batteau.

On certain stretches of quiet water it was easy work. The big boat, pointed at both ends, skimmed along merrily, while from six happy throats came boating songs:

Row, brothers, row, the stream runs fast,
The Rapids are near and the daylight's past —

Rapids were always near, and they created a problem. Some were navigated by poling the boat with twelve-foot spruce poles, tipped with iron, the water "rushing and roaring around." Some were too swift and steep for such a method, so it was necessary to carry the heavy boat and all their gear around the cascade, over the rocky portage.

Thoreau's writing fairly sings as he tells of this

rough voyage through the unspoiled wilderness, fresh with balsam and bayberry. Along the wooded shores the moss made a thick green carpet, and ferns and flowers were everywhere.

Sometimes a fish hawk swooped to catch a trout; then a bald eagle might attack the fish hawk to steal its hard-won dinner. White-throated sparrows sang cheerily. And, to all the other music of the woods, the river added its own deep voice as it ran singing toward the sea.

At night they pitched their camp, making their mattresses of spruce and cedar boughs. Always they lit a fire to last the night. Often they tried their luck at fishing.

Not until they reached the foot of Mount Katahdin, however, where the clean, swift waters of the Abol Stream pour into the Penobscot did they find a rapids so alive with trout that they could be tossed ashore, one after another, through the pine-scented air.

"The speckled trout, and the silvery roaches, swallowed the bait as fast as we could throw in; and the finest specimens of both that I have ever seen."

One fisherman who had lost his hook stood on the shore to help land these fish "as they fell in a perfect shower around him, — sometimes, wet and slippery, full in his face."

Thoreau and his friends might have spent the whole night at this sport. But soon they heard the rough voice of Uncle George, commander of the frying pan: "Send over what you've got. . . . The pork sizzles and cries for fish."

Lying on his bed that night, Thoreau thought it must have been a dream. So he slipped from the tent while his companions were sleeping to test the truth of such fishing.

"There stood Katahdin . . . in the moonlight; and the rippling of the rapids was the only sound to break the stillness. Standing on the shore, I once more cast my line into the stream, and found the dream to be real and the fable true. The speckled trout and silvery roach, like flying-fish, sped swiftly through the moonlight air, describing bright arcs on the dark side of Katahdin." In time the moonlight faded into daylight, and Thoreau, who had caught all the trout that were needed, was willing to put aside his fish pole and start thinking about breakfast.

That day they climbed boulder-strewn Mount Katahdin, the highest peak in Maine, rising a full mile above sea level. They labored up and up through the mountain air. Everywhere were tracks of moose, with now and then the tracks of bear. Much of the way they followed a stream which came cascading toward them down a rocky

ravine — the water as clear as the air itself. At last they stopped to cook some of the many trout they had brought with them, roasting the fish over a glowing fire. Up and up they climbed through blueberries, heavy with fruit; through birch, spruce, fir, and mountain ash, up the deep, narrow ravine "sloping . . . to the clouds."

They slept that night not far from the peak, and the next morning looked out upon the forest far below, spread like an enormous green lawn. So many silver lakes and rivers were scattered over that emerald carpet that they seemed a "mirror broken into a thousand fragments." And in all those forest waters one might find swift trout eager for the lure.

"Time," said Thoreau, "is but the stream I go a-fishing in."

On his two later trips to Maine, Thoreau traveled in each case with only one white companion plus an Indian guide. He had always been fascinated by Indians, and on these canoe trips he constantly questioned them. From these Penobscot woodsmen he learned a few words of their native tongue, how they hunted moose and bear, and how these wilderness dwellers used the herbs and trees of the forest in their daily lives. Almost every root, berry, and leaf had its medicinal value. The black-spruce root could be split into the thinnest and strongest of threads.

Perhaps the birch had more uses than any

other tree. From it one could make torches, pipes, dishes, and paper for writing letters. Best of all, its bark furnished an excellent covering for the feather-light, birch-bark canoes which floated like white swans upon the blue water.

The making of "birches," as these canoes were called, is now virtually a lost art. But when Thoreau visited Maine over a century ago he was able to learn the whole process. First one must search miles of forest for a huge and perfect canoe-birch tree. Then with great care the bark must be removed in a single piece. Building the cedar framework is a difficult and painstaking job as is the shaping of the bark over the cedar frame. Spruce roots or other native fibers are used to sew the ends of the canoe, and gum from evergreens is used to pitch the seams watertight. When finished, the Indian's birch-bark canoe is one of the finest lightweight craft ever invented, easy to guide through the water and to carry over the portage.

On the trip which Thoreau took in 1853, his white companion and Indian guide were determined to get a moose. Thoreau had long since ceased to hunt. He felt it was cruel to take the life of innocent forest creatures merely for "sport." But Thoreau wished to see Maine again, so he came along, without a gun, as "chaplain" to the hunters.

As they glided in their canoe down the Penobscot River, belted kingfishers plunged into the water and came up with small, gleaming fish, wood thrushes spoke their liquid notes, flycatchers and peewees darted after insects, while the handsome wood ducks (which Thoreau called "Summer Ducks") showed colors rivaling even the hummingbird.

Soon there were many evidences of moose: their deep tracks in the mud; water lilies freshly cropped by their browsing.

Joe, the Indian guide, moved cautiously now. They were in good moose country and might come upon one of these enormous, wide-horned animals at any bend in the river. On a certain evening they made camp on an island, stored their baggage, and went moose-hunting.

"At starlight we dropped down the stream . . .
Joe telling us that we must be very silent, and he
himself making no noise with his paddle."

Soon a harvest moon arose. "The lofty, spiring
tops of the spruce and fir were very black against
the sky. . . . A bat flew over our heads." The
drowsy notes of sleepy birds were heard from
time to time.

The river here was "dead water" — slow and
silent as the grave. Even the plunge of a muskrat

into the stream was startling in such stillness. The music of a rill cascading into the river was clearly heard.

At length they turned aside into a creek appropriately called the Moosehorn. This was a meandering stream twenty or thirty feet wide, but comparatively deep. They paddled silently up this tributary between the tall, dark evergreens which "towered on both sides in the moonlight." Narrow meadows furnished excellent

pastures where the moose might graze.

Again and again the Indian guide called the moose through a horn he had made of birch bark. *Ugh-ugh-ugh* . . . *oo — oo — oo — oo.* It was a haunting sound, much like the call of the moose himself echoing through the silent wilderness. They waited, breathless, for an answering call and the rush of a moose through the forest. Once a tree fell with a great sigh and a resounding crash. Thoreau thought for a moment it was a moose. "We saw, many times, what to our imaginations looked like a gigantic moose, with his horns, peering from out the forest edge." But these were only shadows, or the limbs of trees.

A wisp of fog now drifted over the water. Above them, however, the sky was fine and clear as they paddled home to their island in the river. They had seen no moose that night, but they could enjoy the great fire they kindled with its sparks shooting upward toward the stars.

Next morning the ground was white with frost. They breakfasted on tea, bread, and wild ducks, and were soon paddling down the Penobscot, still eager to see moose. About two o'clock they turned up another small stream and upon reaching a meadow heard a crackling of twigs.

"We suddenly spied two moose . . . looking round the alders at us. . . . They made me think of great frightened rabbits, with their long ears and half-inquisitive, half-frightened looks."

While Thoreau and the Indian leaned low in the canoe, Thoreau's companion fired twice over their heads, hitting both the mother moose and her big calf. The mother raced for the forest, but turned to look back at her wounded calf which was following. Then both disappeared into the trees.

The calf was never found, but they soon found the dead mother lying in the stream. Of this huge animal, Joe took only the skin, the tongue, and a little of the meat.

"On more accounts than one," wrote Thoreau, "I had had enough of moose-hunting . . . this hunting of the moose merely for the satisfaction of killing him . . . is too much like going out by night to some wood-side pasture and shooting your neighbor's horses. These are God's own horses, poor, timid creatures, that will run fast enough as soon as they smell you, though they *are* nine feet high."

"This afternoon's experience," wrote Thoreau, "suggested to me how base . . . are the motives which commonly carry men into the wilderness . . . they have no more love for wild nature than wood-sawyers have for forests. . . . For one that comes with a pencil to sketch or sing, a thousand come with an axe or rifle."

Thoreau knew that unless we protect our forests, our wild flowers, our birds, and our animals, there will one day be nothing left of the American wilderness which once stretched its green loveliness from the coast of Maine to the coast of California.

To Make a Better World

8

ONE AFTERNOON, when Thoreau was still living at Walden Pond, he walked to Concord to have a shoe mended. As he reached the village he was arrested by his neighbor Sam Staples, the friendly Concord jailkeeper. Sam was sorry to lock up Thoreau, but he had no choice.

What was Thoreau's offense? He had refused to pay his small poll tax. Sam Staples offered to loan him a dollar if he needed it, but Thoreau was stubborn. He said he would not provide a single penny that might be used in fighting the Mexican War. Thoreau thought that this particular war was an unjust aggression against our southern neighbors, and he was having no part of it, even if it meant going to jail.

Thousands of other American citizens agreed with Thoreau. Abraham Lincoln, while in the House of Representatives, made vigorous protests against the war. Many who hated slavery, feared that any land we might take from Mexico would become slave territory.

Thoreau was not a tax dodger. He was not trying to defraud the government of a trifling sum of money. He was protesting against a national policy which seemed to him to be evil.

It is probably not true that Ralph Waldo Emerson came to the jail to look in through the bars and say:

"Henry, why are you there?"

Whereupon Thoreau is supposed to have replied:

"Waldo, why are you not here?"

But all this might easily have happened in lively Concord where many citizens had independent notions.

Thoreau spent one night in jail, sharing a clean

cell with a man who had been accused of burning a barn. Next morning a veiled woman, probably one of Thoreau's aunts, came to pay the poll tax. The barred door was unlocked. Thoreau was free to pick up his mended shoe and lead a previously planned huckleberry party.

If Thoreau had been a common vagrant, his night in a village jail would long since have been forgotten. But Thoreau was no vagrant. His essay on this experience, entitled "Civil Disobedience," has given courage to free men everywhere. Like Thomas Jefferson, Thoreau believed that the least government is the best government. A nation of Thoreaus might be troublesome to govern. But no nation of such honorable men would ever become a dictatorship.

As Thoreau grew older he modified some of his views:

While young he seldom cooperated with others. It took him most of his life to begin to realize that to have a better world we must work together — at least part of the time, and on certain projects.

Early in life he scoffed at helping the needy.

He admitted that "the mass of men live lives of quiet desperation." But he felt that the way to cure this trouble was to cut expenses to the bone as he had done at Walden Pond. He thought that the best thing one can give the poor is one's "example."

Later in life Thoreau took pity on a small boy whose broken shoes let in the snow and whose ragged clothes were no protection against the bitter winter weather. He bought this grateful boy a warm coat and other clothing.

Thoreau needed solitude. But he also needed friends and neighbors (more than he would ever admit). He dined out frequently. He lectured, and hoped for applause. During one season he managed the Concord Lyceum, securing the lecturers for the entire winter's program. Slowly he was learning to cooperate.

Perhaps his greatest immediate service to Concord was in his role as surveyor. Not only did he continue to "lay out" farms, village lots, and country roads, but in time he became an expert on the flow of the Concord River and its tributaries. Upon his surveys and soundings of these waters was based the legal case of the farmers against the millowners whose dams had flooded and ruined the valuable hay meadows along the river.

After the publication of *Walden,* Thoreau became something of a celebrity. His strange ways were now looked upon with affectionate amusement. And as others grew more tolerant toward Thoreau, he grew more tolerant toward others.

Always fond of animals and children, he now widened his approval. He liked the one-eyed fisherman, Goodwin. He was particularly fond of an old "poetical farmer" named Minott, who when asked if finally he was ready to die said, "No, I've toughed it through the winter, and I want to stay and hear the bluebirds once more."

Thoreau was interested in the Irish who had come to build the Fitchburg railroad, and to work small Concord farms. He liked the answer one such cabin dweller gave him when asked about his potato crop. Said this honest man, "I scratch away, and let the day's work praise itself."

On another occasion he was entertained by four youngsters and a horse:

"I am amused to see four little Irish boys only five or six years old getting a horse in a pasture. . . . They have all in a row got hold of a very long halter and are leading him. All wish to have a hand in it. It is surprising that he obeys such small specimens of humanity, but he seems to be very docile, a real family horse. At length, by dint of pulling and shouting, they get him into a run down a hill, and though he moves very deliberately, scarcely faster than a walk, all but the one at the end of the line soon cut and run to right and left, without having looked behind, expecting him to be upon them. They haul up at last at the bars . . . and then the family puppy . . . comes bounding to join them and assist. He is as youthful and about as knowing as any of them. The horse marches gravely behind, obeying the faint tug at the halter. . . . It is interesting to behold this faithful beast, the oldest and wisest of the company, thus implicitly obeying the lead of the youngest and weakest."

At long last Thoreau was beginning to like people as much as he liked woodchucks, wild ducks, and chickadees.

Meanwhile he walked and talked with Ellery Channing and other intelligent Concord friends. He delighted in the salty and spry conversation of Aunt Mary Emerson, still a small bundle of bursting energy.

To Concord came such distinguished men as Louis Agassiz, the Swiss-American naturalist, and the elder Henry James. Thoreau met them all, usually at Emerson's.

A Concord visitor of a different and wilder sort was John Brown, the bearded abolitionist. Brown and his sons had been fighting the slavery faction in Kansas in those days of tumult leading to the Civil War. Fanatical though this crusader may have been, his honesty and bravery appealed to Thoreau. When Brown later launched his unsuccessful raid on Harpers Ferry, and faced hanging as a consequence, Thoreau made his "Plea for Captain John Brown" — a lecture which created great excitement in Concord and wherever else it was repeated. The gentle hermit of Walden Pond was beginning to realize that to improve this world we must not only cooperate, but at times cooperate forcefully.

Thoreau sought greater freedom for all men everywhere. Certainly the slaves must be freed; but so must workers in the "dark Satanic mills"; so must the farmer, painfully harnessed to his farm and his mortgage; so must the villager and the city dweller, blind to the beauties of nature.

One way to free man is to lure him outdoors. And for this purpose there must be parks and recreation areas.

Thoreau was one of the first true conservationists in America. "Each town should have a park," he wrote, "or rather a primitive forest, of five hundred or a thousand acres . . . a common possession forever."

Decades before the average American gave any thought to such problems, Thoreau realized that the forests were being destroyed, the pastures overgrazed and the fields eroded. He himself had lived to see the destruction of the white-pine forests of Maine. Soon would come a similar destruction in Michigan and Wisconsin. Even today we struggle to save a few giant redwoods and Douglas firs on the Pacific coast.

"Every creature is better alive than dead," wrote Thoreau, "men and moose and pine-trees."

Many years before our national government set aside its first acre of virgin wilderness, Thoreau was asking, "Why should not we have our national preserves? . . . not for idle sport or food, but for inspiration and our own true recreation!"

Slowly America awakens to the fact that Thoreau of Walden was one of our wisest prophets.

The Autumn Years

9

IF THOREAU had so desired, he might have become modestly wealthy. He had invented a secret process for grinding graphite into the smoothest powder of its kind available in America. Printing companies used quantities of this powder in the manufacture of electrotypes. They were willing to pay a premium for Thoreau graphite.

Henry had always aided his father. When the old gentleman died on February 3, 1859, his son took over the management of the business, and the family fortunes continued to improve. Thoreau, however, suffered a heavy penalty for his hours in the shop. Into his lungs he was

breathing more and more of the dangerous
graphite dust.

"I think that I cannot preserve my health and
spirits," he wrote, "unless I spend four hours a
day at least . . . sauntering through the woods and
over the hills and fields, absolutely free from all
worldly engagements. . . ."

Bracing air was to be found at the summit of
Mount Monadnock, which Thoreau continued to
climb. Here he was above all dust — cloud-high,
bird-high, and far from the demands of his
business.

Even in his leisure, however, Thoreau de-
manded too much of his body, sleeping outdoors
in all sorts of weather. Frequently he was soaked
by rain and chilled by the night air. Perhaps he
loved the woods and water "not wisely, but too
well."

It was during one of his usual walks on a cold
December day in 1860 that he caught the severe
"bronchitis" which eventually led to his death.
He had been counting the annual rings on some
trees which had been sawed down. Later he stood

in the street arguing with a friend.

Medication failed to ease his cough or aid his weak condition. Even a trip to Minnesota for his health proved of little benefit. He continued to keep his journal until November 3, 1861 — the last entry describing the results of a violent autumn storm.

A narrow rattan day bed which he himself had constructed was brought down from his bedroom so that he could spend more time with his family. And on this pallet lay Henry David Thoreau — the best walker and mountain climber in Concord — scarcely able to rise from his couch.

While any strength remained, however, he continued to work on three long articles which had been commissioned by the editor of the *Atlantic Monthly*.

One of these essays, entitled "Walking," recalled the happy years he had spent wandering the back woods and woodland paths. Thoreau was speaking for "absolute freedom and wildness," and he made a good case for the life he loved.

Another was called "Autumnal Tints." In this

he mixed his colors with the skill of a good land-scape painter to show the sudden beauty of New England, swept by the icy flame of the first frost.

Finest of these prose poems is "Wild Apples," an essay spiked with the tart tang of Henry Thoreau himself, who admired the vagrant fruit trees to be found in old hedgerows and pastures. Wild apples, he observed, "should be eaten in the fields, when your system is all aglow with exercise, when the frosty weather nips your fingers, the wind rattles the bare boughs or rustles the few remaining leaves, and the jay bird is heard screaming around. . . . Some of these apples might be labeled, 'To be eaten in the wind.'"

Thoreau had lived less than 45 years. He had hoped to live long enough to complete several more books. But autumn came early to this lover of autumn. He remained cheerful and uncomplaining to the end.

To one who asked his opinion on life beyond the grave, Thoreau could only whisper, "One world at a time." To an aunt, who inquired whether he had made his peace with God, he answered gently that he was unaware they had ever quarreled.

Sam Staples, his one-time jailer, came to pay his last respects. Sam reported to Emerson that he had "never spent an hour with more satisfaction. Never saw a man dying with so much pleasure and peace."

Orchards were in bloom on that morning of May 6, 1862. One friend came with a dish of jelly. Another brought a bouquet of flowers which carried a breath of spring into the room.

Two hours later Thoreau asked to be lifted up on his bed — perhaps to see the apple trees beyond the window. And so he died, quietly and apparently without pain.

Emerson, speaking sadly, gave the funeral oration. He mentioned the failings as well as the virtues of this stubborn, honorable man:

"It was a pleasure and a privilege to walk with him. He knew the country like a fox or a bird. . . . His eye was open to beauty, and his ear to music. . . . His soul was made for the noblest

society. . . . Wherever there is knowledge, wherever there is virtue, wherever there is beauty, he will find a home."

Louisa Alcott of Concord also felt the loss of this strange and brilliant neighbor. And she, like Emerson, paid tribute to his memory:

> Spring comes to us in guise forlorn;
> The bluebird chants a requiem;
> The willow-blossom waits for him; —
> The Genius of the wood is gone.

Thoreau's body lies beside those of Emerson and Lidian Emerson, and the members of his own beloved family in Sleepy Hollow Cemetery in Concord. But the words he wrote are still alive. He walks beside countless thousands whenever they saunter through the woods or meadows. His spirit will never die. It will return each spring while there are meadow larks and hyacinths.

A Walden Calendar

I⊤ IS NOT enough to read a book *about* Thoreau.
One must then go on to read the writings of the
man himself: first *Walden,* then *A Week on the
Concord and Merrimack Rivers,* and finally his
essays, travel sketches, and journals. These are
pleasures which you will wish to spread over
many years, for Thoreau is a writer to be sampled
and savored.

The following calendar is an arrangement of
excerpts from Thoreau's best and best-known
book, *Walden.* It is to be hoped that this circling
of the year, from Spring through Summer,
Autumn, and Winter and back to Spring again
will give the reader a taste of Thoreau's genius,
and a hunger to read his works.

S P R I N G

I long ago lost a hound, a bay horse, and a turtledove, and am still on their trail. Many are the travellers I have spoken concerning them, describing their tracks and what calls they answer to. I have met one or two who had heard the hound, and the tramp of the horse, and even seen the dove disappear behind a cloud, and they seemed as anxious to recover them as if they had lost them themselves.

Near the end of March, 1845, I borrowed an axe and went down to the woods by Walden Pond, nearest to where I intended to build my house, and began to cut down some tall, arrowy white pines, still in their youth, for timber. . . . The owner of the axe, as he released his hold on it, said that it was the apple of his eye; but I returned it sharper than I received it. It was a pleasant hillside where I worked, covered with pine woods, through which I looked out on the pond, and a small open field in the woods where pines and hickories were springing up. The ice in the pond was not yet dissolved ... but ... I heard the lark and pewee and other birds already come to commence another year with us. They were pleasant spring days, in which the winter of man's discontent was thawing as well as the earth ... I heard a stray goose groping about over the pond ... like the spirit of the fog.

By the middle of April, for I made no haste in

my work . . . my house was framed and ready for the raising. . . . I dug my cellar in the side of a hill sloping to the south, where a woodchuck had formerly dug his burrow, down through sumach and blackberry roots, and the lowest stain of vegetation, six feet square by seven deep, to a fine sand where potatoes would not freeze in any winter. . . . It was but two hours' work.

At length, in the beginning of May, with the help of some of my acquaintances . . . I set up the

frame of my house. No man was ever more honored in the character of his raisers than I.

S U M M E R

I began to occupy my house on the 4th of July, as soon as it was boarded and roofed . . . I laid the foundation of a chimney at one end, bringing two cartloads of stones up the hill from the pond. . . .

I would observe, by the way, that it costs me nothing for curtains, for I have no gazers to shut out but the sun and the moon, and I am willing that they should look in.

I found myself suddenly neighbor to the birds . . . the wood thrush, the veery, the scarlet tanager, the field sparrow, the whip-poor-will, and many others.

From a hill-top near by, where the wood had been recently cut off, there was a pleasing vista

southward across the pond, through a wide in-
dentation in the hills which form the shore there.
. . . That way I looked between and over the near
green hills to some distant and higher ones in the
horizon, tinged with blue. Indeed, by standing
on tiptoe I could catch a glimpse of some of the
peaks of the still bluer and more distant mountain
ranges in the northwest, those true-blue coins
from heaven's own mint. . . .

Every morning was a cheerful invitation to
make my life of equal simplicity, and I may say
innocence, with Nature herself. I have been as
sincere a worshipper of Aurora as the Greeks. I
got up early and bathed in the pond; that was a
religious exercise, and one of the best things
which I did.

Time is but the stream I go a-fishing in. I drink
at it; but while I drink I see the sandy bottom
and detect how shallow it is. Its thin current
slides away, but eternity remains. I would drink
deeper; fish in the sky, whose bottom is pebbly
with stars.

No wonder that Alexander carried the Iliad
with him on his expeditions in a precious casket.
A written word is the choicest of relics.

I love a broad margin to my life. Sometimes, in
a summer morning, having taken my accustomed
bath, I sat in my sunny doorway from sunrise till
noon ... in undisturbed solitude and stillness,
while the birds sang around or flitted noiseless
through the house.... I grew in those seasons

like corn in the night. . . . My days were not days of the week . . . nor were they minced into hours and fretted by the ticking of a clock. . . . This was sheer idleness to my fellow-townsmen, no doubt; but if the birds and flowers had tried me by their standard, I should not have been found wanting.

Housework was a pleasant pastime. When my floor was dirty, I rose early, and, setting all my furniture out of doors on the grass . . . dashed water on the floor, and sprinkled white sand from the pond on it, and then with a broom scrubbed it clean and white.

As I sit at my window this summer afternoon, hawks are circling about my clearing; the tantivity of wild pigeons, flying by twos and threes athwart my view, or perching restless on the white pine boughs behind my house, gives a voice to the air; a fish hawk dimples the glassy surface of the pond and brings up a fish; a mink steals out of the marsh before my door and seizes a frog by the shore; the sedge is bending under the weight of the reed-birds . . . and for the last half-hour I have heard the rattle of railroad cars, now dying away and then reviving like the beat of a partridge, conveying travelers from Boston to the country.

Regularly at half-past seven, in one part of the summer, after the evening train had gone by, the whip-poor-wills chanted their vespers for half an hour, sitting on a stump by my door, or upon the ridge-pole of the house. . . . When other birds are still, the screech owls take up the strain, like mourning women. . . . Late in the evening I heard the distant rumbling of wagons over bridges, — a sound heard farther than almost any other at night. . . . In the meanwhile all the shore rang with the trump of bullfrogs, the sturdy spirits of ancient wine-bibbers and wassailers . . . *tr-r-r-oonk, tr-r-r-oonk, tr-r-r-oonk!*

The mice which haunted my house were not the common ones . . . and would run over my shoes and up my clothes . . . and round and round the paper which held my dinner. . . . A phoebe soon built in my shed. . . . In June the partridge . . . which is so shy a bird, led her brood past my windows . . . clucking and calling to them like a hen.

A U T U M N

In the fall the loon . . . came, as usual . . . making the woods ring with his wild laughter. . . . When I went to get a pail of water early in the

morning I frequently saw this stately bird sailing
out of my cove. . . . If I endeavored to overtake
him in a boat, in order to see how he would
manoeuvre, he would dive and be completely
lost, so that I did not discover him again, sometimes, till the latter part of the day. . . . It was a
pretty game, played on the smooth surface of
the pond, a man against a loon.

In October I went a-graping to the river

meadows, and loaded myself with clusters more precious for their beauty and fragrance than for food. There, too, I admired, though I did not gather, the cranberries, small waxen gems, pendants of the meadow grass, pearly and red, which the farmer plucks with an ugly rake, leaving the smooth meadow in a snarl, heedlessly measuring them by the bushel and the dollar only. . . . The barberry's brilliant fruit was likewise food for my eyes merely; but I collected a small store of wild

apples for coddling, which the proprietor and travellers had overlooked. When chestnuts were ripe I laid up half a bushel for winter. It was very exciting at that season to roam the then boundless chestnut woods . . . with a bag on my shoulder, and a stick to open burs with in my hand . . . amid the rustling of leaves and the loud reproofs of the red squirrels and the jays. . . .

Already, by the first of September, I had seen two or three small maples turned scarlet across the pond. . . . Ah, many a tale their color told!

The wasps came by thousands to my lodge in October, as to winter quarters, and settled on my windows within and on the walls overhead, sometimes deterring visitors from entering.

I did not plaster till it was freezing weather. I brought over some whiter and cleaner sand for this purpose from the opposite shore of the pond in a boat. . . . My house had in the meanwhile been shingled down to the ground on every side. . . . I admired anew the economy and convenience of plastering, which so efficiently shuts out the cold and takes a handsome finish. . . .

The first ice is especially interesting and perfect, being hard, dark, and transparent, and affords the best opportunity that ever offers for examining the bottom . . . for you can lie at your length . . . and study the bottom at your leisure . . . like a picture behind a glass.

W I N T E R

At length the winter set in in good earnest, just as I had finished plastering, and the wind began to howl around the house as if it had not had permission to do so till then. Night after night the geese came lumbering in in the dark with a clangor and a whistling of wings, even after the ground was covered with snow, some to alight in Walden, and some flying low over the woods . . . bound for Mexico. . . . In 1845 Walden froze entirely over for the first time on the night of the 22d of December.

I withdrew yet farther into my shell, and endeavored to keep a bright fire both within my house and within my breast. My employment out of doors now was to collect the dead wood in the forest . . . sometimes trailing a dead pine tree under each arm to my shed. An old forest fence which had seen its best days was a great haul for me. . . . How much more interesting an event is that man's supper who has just been forth in the snow to hunt . . . the fuel to cook it with.

Every man looks at his wood-pile with a kind
of affection. I love to have mine before my
window, and the more chips the better to remind
me of my pleasing work. . . . I played about the
stumps which I had got out of my bean-field . . .
they warmed me twice, — once while I was split-
ting them, and again when they were on the fire.
. . . A few pieces of fat pine were a great treasure.

Go thou my incense upward from this hearth,
And ask the gods to pardon this clear flame.

The moles nested in my cellar, nibbling every third potato, and making a snug bed . . . for even the wildest animals love comfort and warmth as well as man, and they survive the winter only because they are so careful to secure them.

I weathered some merry snow-storms, and spent some cheerful winter evenings by my fireside, while the snow whirled wildly without, and even the hooting of the owl was hushed. For many weeks I met no one in my walks but those who came occasionally to cut wood and sled it to the village.

I frequently tramped eight or ten miles through the deepest snow to keep an appointment with a beech tree, or a yellow birch, or an old acquaintance among the pines. . . .

Sometimes I heard the foxes as they ranged over the snow-crust, in moonlight nights, in search of a partridge or other game, barking raggedly and demonically like forest dogs. . . . Usually the red squirrel . . . waked me in the dawn, coursing over the roof and up and down the sides of the house. . . . I threw out half a bushel of ears of sweet corn . . . and was amused by watching . . . the various animals which were baited by it. In the twilight and the night the rabbits came regularly and made a hearty meal. All day long the red squirrels came and went. . . . At length the jays arrive, whose discordant screams were heard long before, as they were warily making their approach. . . . They were manifestly thieves, and I had not much respect for them. . . .

Meanwhile also came the chickadees in flocks . . . to pick a dinner out of my wood-pile, or the crumbs at my door, with faint flitting lisping notes, like the tinkling of icicles in the grass, or else with sprightly *day day day,* or more rarely, in spring-like days, a wiry summery *phe-be* from the wood-side. They were so familiar that at length one alighted on an armful of wood which I was carrying in, and pecked at the sticks without fear.

SPRING AGAIN

One attraction in coming to the woods to live was that I should have leisure and opportunity to see the Spring come in. The ice in the pond at length begins to be honeycombed. . . . Fogs and rains and warmer suns are gradually melting the snow. . . . I am on the alert for the first signs of spring, to hear the chance note of some arriving bird. . . . On the 13th of March, after I had heard

the bluebird, song sparrow, and red-wing, the ice was still nearly a foot thick.

At the approach of spring the red squirrels got under my house, two at a time, directly under my feet as I sat reading or writing, and kept up the queerest chuckling and chirruping and vocal pirouetting and gurgling sounds that ever were heard; and when I stamped they only chirruped the louder, as if past all fear and respect in their

mad pranks. . . . They were wholly deaf to my arguments. . . .

The grass flames up on the hillsides like a spring fire . . . not yellow but green is the color of its flame. . . .

Walden is melting apace. . . . A great field of ice has cracked off the main body. I hear a song sparrow singing from the bushes on the shore, — *olit, olit, olit,* — *chip, chip, chip, che char,* — *che wiss, wiss, wiss.* He too is helping to crack it.

I heard a robin in the distance, the first I had heard for many a thousand years, methought, whose note I shall not forget for many a thousand more, — the same sweet and powerful song. . . . O the evening robin, at the end of a New England summer day!

. . . the sun shines bright and warm this first spring morning, re-creating the world. . . .

On the 29th of April, as I was fishing from the

bank of the river near the Nine-Acre-Corner bridge, standing on the quaking grass and willow roots, where the muskrats lurk . . . I observed a very slight and graceful hawk . . . showing the under side of its wings, which gleamed like a satin ribbon in the sun, or like the pearly inside of a shell. . . . Beside this I got a rare mess of golden and silver and bright cupreous fishes, which looked like a string of jewels. Ah! I have penetrated to those meadows on the morning of many a first spring day, jumping from hummock to hummock, from willow root to willow root, when the wild river valley and the woods were bathed in so pure and bright a light as would have waked the dead. . . . There needs no stronger proof of immortality.

And so another spring rolled on toward another summer. And Henry David Thoreau left his cabin on the shore of Walden "for as good a reason" as he came, perhaps because he had "several more lives to live." But for his tens of thousands of readers and admirers he still haunts that woodland lake, still plays his flute by moonlight, hoes his beans, and cooks his evening meal over an open fire. The wild geese and chickadees, the lark and the thrush know this is true. Each year they visit Walden, keeping their appointment as faithfully as Thoreau once kept his.

Index